China's Energy Security in the Twenty-First Century

Studies of the Contemporary Asia Pacific (SCAP)
This series is the flagship publication of the London Asia Pacific Centre for Social Science, based at SOAS, University of London and King's College London. 'Peace and prosperity' have underpinned the Asia-Pacific region's rise in the international system since the end of the Cold War. This series seeks to understand the contemporary challenges to 'peace and prosperity'. In particular, it seeks to understand the origins and dynamics of three issues: the divergence between economic and social development along with the worsening of relative disparities, the global constraints facing the region's export-led growth model, and the persistence of interstate conflicts. Based on these comparative and international guiding themes, this series seeks to publish original monographs and edited volumes on the Asia-Pacific, irrespective of the methodological approach.

Series Editors
Tat Yan Kong (School of Oriental and African Studies, University of London), Ramon Pacheco Pardo (King's College London, University of London)

Editorial Board
Dafydd Fell (School of Oriental and African Studies, University of London), Charlotte Goodburn (King's College London, University of London), Nahee Kang (King's College London, University of London), Costas Lapavitsas (School of Oriental and African Studies, University of London), Andrew Sumner (King's College London, University of London), Ulrich Volz (School of Oriental and African Studies, University of London)

International Advisory Panel
Yin-Wah Chu (Hong Kong Baptist University), Jane Duckett (University of Glasgow), Megan Greene (University of Kansas), Eunmee Kim (Ewha Woman's University), Syaru Shirley Lin (University of Virginia), Danny Quah (National University of Singapore), Jeffrey Reeves (Asia Pacific Foundation of Canada), Joseph Wong (University of Toronto), Meredith Woo (Sweet Briar College), Hosoya Yuichi (Keio University), Ariel Yusuf (Padjhajharan University), Feng Zhang (South China University of Technology)

Books in the Series
China's Energy Security in the Twenty-First Century: The Role of Global Governance and Climate Change
Kaho Yu

New Asian Disorder: Rivalries Embroiling the Pacific Century
Edited by Lowell Dittmer

China's Energy Security in the Twenty-First Century

The Role of Global Governance and Climate Change

Kaho Yu

Hong Kong University Press
The University of Hong Kong
Pok Fu Lam Road
Hong Kong
https://hkupress.hku.hk

© 2023 Hong Kong University Press

ISBN 978-988-8805-63-1 (*Hardback*)

The author is grateful to the following publishers for their permission to adapt his previously published work in this book:

Chapter 1 was adapted from: Kaho Yu, 'What about Climate? China's Energy Transition and the War in Ukraine', in *The Future of Xi's China: Scenarios and Implications for Europe*, edited by Alessia Amighini, ISPI, 2022.

Chapter 2 was adapted from: Kaho Yu, 'Energy Cooperation in the Belt and Road Initiative: EU Experience of the Trans-European Networks for Energy', *Asia Europe Journal* 16 (3) (2018): 251–265, adapted by permission from RightsLink Printable License: Springer Nature; and Kaho Yu, 'Energy Cooperation under the Belt and Road Initiative: Implications for Global Energy Governance', *Journal of World Investment & Trade* 20 (2–3) (2019): 243–258, available online at https://brill.com/view/journals/jwit/20/2-3/article-p243_3.xml?rskey=DDjHHE&result=1.

Chapter 4 was adapted from: Kaho Yu and Yunheng Zhou, 'China's Energy Security and Sino-African Energy Cooperation', in *China's Energy Security: A Multidimensional Perspective*, edited by Giulia Romano and Jean-Francois Meglio, © 2016 and Imprint. Reproduced by permission of Taylor & Francis Group.

All rights reserved. No portion of this publication may be reproduced or transmitted in any form or by any means, electronic or mechanical, including photocopying, recording, or any information storage or retrieval system, without prior permission in writing from the publisher.

British Library Cataloguing-in-Publication Data
A catalogue record for this book is available from the British Library.

Digitally printed

Contents

Foreword by Professor Keunwook Paik	vii
Foreword by Professor Xia Yishan	viii
Foreword by Professor Ramon Pacheco Pardo	x
Acknowledgements	xii
List of Abbreviations	xiii
Introduction	1
A Debate of Chinese Energy Security	3
Structure of the Subsequent Chapters	6
1. Evolution of Chinese Energy and Climate Strategy: From Going-Out Strategy to the Belt and Road Initiative	8
A Historical Overview of China's Energy Security and Strategy	9
Chinese Energy Strategy: From Energy Diplomacy to Global Energy Governance?	17
2. Belt and Road Initiative, AIIB, and Global Energy Governance	25
Energy Cooperation in the Belt and Road Initiative	25
AIIB and Global Energy Governance	31
China's View towards International Energy Organisations	34
Belt and Road Investment and Global Energy Governance	37
3. China–Central Asia Energy Cooperation: A Transnational Infrastructure Network of Oil and Gas Pipelines	40
China and Central Asia Energy Cooperation	41
China's Energy Diplomacy in Central Asia	48
Chinese Energy Cooperation via the SCO	50
Multilateralism in China–Central Asia Energy Cooperation	53
4. China-Africa Energy Cooperation: From Oil Diplomacy to Low-Carbon Investments	56
China-Africa Energy Cooperation	57
China's Energy Diplomacy in Africa	61
China's Energy Cooperation via the FOCAC	65
Multilateralism in China-Africa Energy Cooperation	70

5. China-EU Energy Cooperation: A Partnership in Low-Carbon
   Transition 72
   The Foundation of China-EU Energy Cooperation 73
   China's Energy Relations with the EU and Its Member States 75
   Energy Cooperation Mechanism between China and the EU 78
   Multilateralism in EU-China Energy Cooperation 83

6. Conclusion: What Is Next for China in Global Energy Governance? 88
   Belt and Road Initiative and the Asia Infrastructure Investment Bank 89
   China–Central Asia Energy Cooperation 90
   China-Africa Energy Cooperation 91
   China-EU Clean Energy Cooperation 92
   Four Challenges China Faces in Global Energy Governance 93
   What Is Next? 96

Appendix 101
Bibliography 113

Foreword

China's growing role in global energy and climate governance ranks among the most pressing subjects in international relations of the twenty-first century. How will China's global energy hunt and climate pledges impact the world? What are the implications for global energy markets? What are the geopolitical consequences?

Dr Kaho Yu's book is an excellent contribution to understanding China's energy strategy, particularly how it uses global governance to carry out its energy and climate strategies. Kaho takes a multi-disciplinary approach to unpack the complicated interlinkage of Chinese energy security, climate politics, and foreign policy. It provides an in-depth empirical analysis of Chinese energy and climate policies over the last two decades and the mechanisms of China's international energy cooperation.

Universities are beginning to see the need to offer more energy and climate programmes. Energy companies are evaluating the material impacts driven by geopolitics and climate change. International organisations are also trying to find a way to accommodate China's demand. The arrival of Kaho's book is perfectly timed.

As Kaho's mentor, I am pleased to see that Hong Kong University Press values his research on global energy and climate policies over the last decade and has decided to publish it as a book. I have no doubt that this book will help scholars, students, policymakers, and businesses better understand China's energy security, climate politics, and international relations.

This foreword is a special one as I did not have the chance to participate on the examiner panel during the defence of Kaho's PhD thesis.

Professor Keunwook Paik
Author of *Sino-Russian Oil and Gas Cooperation: The Reality and Implications*

Foreword

Energy and climate are interlinked at the forefront of international relations nowadays. Energy itself is a multi-disciplinary subject, covering policy, economic, social, scientific, and climate aspects. Addressing energy and climate issues also requires national, regional, and global perspectives. Therefore, it would be incomprehensive to discuss climate action in isolation from energy structures, analyse energy issues in isolation from climate change, or promote energy and climate cooperation in isolation from diplomatic relations. How to advance sustainable development with an organic integration of the three issues is a pressing topic, and should be confronted seriously by the international community today.

What is valuable about this book is that it is not simply an enumeration of the three issues of energy, climate, and international relations, but also a systematic account of the development of China's international energy strategy. The author provides a theoretical foundation and a global perspective for analysing these three interlinked fields and their interactions. The book offers a detailed overview of the current international energy and climate situation, and of China's role in global energy and climate governance. It also provides an in-depth discussion of energy cooperation along the Belt and Road. Furthermore, it demonstrates the field research and expertise of the author across multiple disciplines, countries, industries, and perspectives.

The author of this book, Dr Yu Kaho, is an extremely talented young scholar whom I have worked with in the past. I was introduced to him by a close friend, Professor Keunwook Paik, from Chatham House, at a conference at the China Institute of International Studies. In addition to his own research and teaching, Kaho served as my assistant, helping me with research and interpretation. We have always maintained a good personal relationship, often discussing topics such as the Belt and Road, international energy cooperation, China-US-Russia relations and global governance, and have attended many domestic and international energy conferences together. I am impressed that many of his judgements on situations in the fields of energy, climate, and international relations have since proved to be accurate.

Foreword

Kaho has always been passionate about academic research, especially on topics related to energy, climate, and international relations. I am delighted that he is working with Hong Kong University Press to compile his research and studies over the past decade into a book. I believe this book is of tremendous value and will help improve the understanding of international energy and climate for both domestic and international readers.

Professor Xia Yishan (夏义善教授)
China Institute of International Studies

Foreword

China is a superpower. It is the second largest economy in the world, with the second most powerful armed forces. It is also a major global investor and donor, as well as a diplomatic juggernaut in different regions. The Chinese government has even started to develop its own institutions and initiatives that are shaking international relations. Whether it is the Belt and Road Initiative, the Asian Infrastructure Investment Bank, or the Forum on China-Africa Cooperation, any initiative that China unveils has global repercussions. We ignore this reality at our peril.

This holds true for China's approach to energy security. Long are the days when China emphasised self-reliance. Following years of high economic growth, China became a net energy importer in the 1990s. This certainly had huge repercussions for China's energy policy. But the Chinese economy's thirst for foreign oil and gas has also affected world energy markets. Whether you are filling up your car's tank in Europe or Sub-Saharan Africa, heating your home in North Africa or Latin America, or working in a factory in East Asia or North America, China's energy policy directly affects you. And this will continue for decades to come.

Yet, how much do we know about China's approach to energy security and how it impacts other parts of the world? The truth is that many analysts and scholars approach Beijing's energy security putting ideology first. 'Neo-colonialism', 'energy imperialism', or 'hunt for energy resources' are some of the terms used by those who believe that China can do no right. 'Win-win' is the term more commonly used by those who think that Beijing can do no wrong. Sobering analysis is replaced by political (energy) football.

In this context, Dr Kaho Yu's is required reading. He offers a nuanced, methodical, and very readable analysis of China's energy security. Having had the opportunity and honour to supervise Kaho's thesis, I can attest that this analysis is the result of years of hard work, perseverance in getting access to interviewees with key information, a careful investigation of relevant archives, and an original interpretation of publicly available resources. This combination makes Kaho's book a unique contribution to our understanding of China's approach to energy security and foreign policy. That is to say, this book helps understand the global politics of the twenty-first century.

Professor Ramon Pacheco Pardo
Professor of International Relations, King's College London

Acknowledgements

Turning my PhD thesis into a book was the best way to record my academic journey.

First, I would like to gratefully and sincerely thank my supervisor, Professor Ramon Pacheco Pardo, for his guidance, understanding, and dedication during my graduate studies at King's College London. His continuous support helped me throughout the process of writing this thesis. I could not have imagined having a better PhD supervisor.

I am incredibly grateful to my mentors, Professor Paik Keunwook and Professor Xia Yishan, for broadening my horizons with their motivation, enthusiasm, and immense knowledge. It has been a privilege to receive their proper and generous guidance in getting my graduate career started on the right foot. I wish to express my deep gratitude for their support and encouragement.

Throughout the research period, I met and worked alongside many great scholars; and fortunately, some have become great friends. I am also grateful to the interviewees who were willing to share their knowledge and experience with me.

My deepest thanks must also go to my family. I could have never completed my PhD thesis without the patience and understanding of my wife Yifei and parents. Our adorable Berry Bear has also brought us the most remarkable joy. Their love and support has allowed me to fulfil my goals and ambitions on my academic journey.

Finally, I would like to extend my gratitude to the Hong Kong University Press team, Professor Tat Yan Kong, and Professor Ramon Pacheco Pardo for publishing my PhD thesis in their Studies of the Contemporary Asia Pacific book series.

It was incredibly rewarding to research and write this book. I hope that readers enjoy it as much as I enjoyed writing it.

Kaho Yu
August 2022

Abbreviations

Abbreviation	Explanation
ADB	Asia Development Bank
AIIB	Asia Infrastructure Investment Bank
ASEAN	Association of Southeast Asian Nations
bcm	billion cubic metres
BIT	bilateral investment treaty
BP	British Petroleum
BRI	Belt and Road Initiative
CCS	carbon dioxide capture and storage
CGNPC	China Guangdong Nuclear Power Corp
CNOC	Chinese national oil company
CNODC	China National Oil and Gas Exploration and Development Corporation
CNOOC	China National Offshore Oil Corporation
CNPC	China National Petroleum Corporation
CPC	Communist Party of China
DG	Directorate-General
EBRD	European Bank for Reconstruction and Development
EC DG ENER	European Commission Directorate-General for Energy
EC2	China-EU Clean Energy Centre
ECT	Energy Charter Treaty
EEC	European Economic Community
EPC	Engineering, procurement, and construction
EU	European Union
FDI	foreign direct investment

Abbreviation	Explanation
FOCAC	Forum on China-Africa Cooperation
HLME	China-EU High-Level Meeting on Energy
ICARE	Institute for Clean and Renewable Energy
IEA	International Energy Agency
IEF	International Energy Forum
IPR	intellectual property rights
IRENA	International Renewable Energy Agency
JEEP	Joint Energy and Environment Programme
KMG	KazMunaiGaz
MFA	Ministry of Foreign Affairs
MLR	Ministry of Land and Resources
MOFCOM	Ministry of Commerce
MOST	Ministry of Science and Technology
NATO	North Atlantic Treaty Organization
NDRC	National Development and Reform Commission
NEA	National Energy Administration
NEC	National Energy Commission
NOC	national oil company
NZEC	Near Zero Emission Coal
OECD	Organization for Economic Cooperation and Development
OPEC	Organization of the Petroleum Exporting Countries
PRC	People Republic of China
R&D	research and development
SAFE	State Administration of Foreign Exchange
SASAC	State-owned Assets Supervision and Administration Commission
SBPCI	State Bureau of Petroleum and Chemical Industry
SCO	Shanghai Cooperation Organisation
SDPC	State Development and Planning Commission
SEC	State Economic Commission
SELG	State Energy Leading Group
SETC	State Economic and Trade Commission
SinoChem	China Chemical Import and Export Company

Abbreviation	Explanation
Sinopec	Sinopec Group
SPC	State Planning Commission
TCC	China Tianchen Engineering Corporation
UNCOAL	Union Oil Company of California
UNDP	United Nations Development Programme
WB	World Bank
WTO	World Trade Organization

Introduction[1]

Energy and climate are interlinked in global affairs. In order to navigate supply disruptions driven by geopolitics and climate change, China has been highlighting international cooperation, in particular global governance, as a key means to enhance its energy security. Over the last two decades, the Chinese leadership has also incorporated global energy and climate governance in China's grand strategies, from the going-out strategy to the Belt and Road Initiative. The way China promotes international cooperation for energy security has impacted global, regional, and national energy markets, with significant geopolitical consequences.

While energy security is a top national interest of China, its scope has evolved over the last few decades. After China became a net oil importer in 1993, it started to diversify its supply by expanding its overseas upstream portfolio via the 'going-out' strategy. In the following two decades, China expanded the scope of energy security by incorporating new elements, particularly the global supply chain, climate change, and global governance. Energy continued to be a core aspect when China rolled out the Belt and Road Initiative (BRI) in 2015, with a more multilateral plan to enhance infrastructure connectivity, commodity trade, supply chain integration, low-carbon development, and international finance. The Paris Agreement, signed in 2016, has driven China towards further contributing to global climate governance. In 2020, when the Chinese leadership called for enhancing energy security due to global supply chain disruptions driven by the China-US trade war, the COVID-19 pandemic, and accelerated energy transition, global energy governance was seen as part of the solution. The rationale underlying the strategy of Chinese energy security has shifted from merely chasing quantitative objectives (e.g., increasing the amount of oil imported) to including some qualitative goals (e.g., improving supply chain diversification, sustainability and governance) that rely on multilateralism. The realisation of the BRI is set

---

1. The views, thoughts, and opinions expressed in this book belong solely to the author, and not necessarily to the author's employer, affiliated organisations, or other group of individuals.

to result in a more multilateral energy strategy for China, one that has the potential to modify and even upend the current global and regional order.

At the global level, China's energy demand has influenced the development of the world's energy markets, climate campaigns, and global governance.[2] At the regional level, Chinese investments have changed the existing structures of energy supply by building new transport infrastructure that connects energy resource bases to the Chinese market.[3] At the national level, Chinese investments have become an important source of capital and technology for developing domestic energy infrastructure and energy transition in China's partner countries.[4]

While there is criticism that China is adopting an aggressive energy diplomacy stance to increase its power in the international system,[5] the Chinese government has argued that it actively engages in global energy governance to contribute to the stability of the global energy market. China's grand strategy, the Belt and Road Initiative,[6] and a number of Chinese policy agendas, such as the Energy White Paper in 2007, 2012, and 2020 and the Action Plan for Carbon Dioxide Peaking Before 2030,[7] have emphasised multilateral approaches and global energy governance as a means of enhancing international energy cooperation. To date, China has actively promoted energy and climate cooperation in several international organisations and participated in various international energy organisations. Beyond these organisations, China has also promoted global energy governance via regional initiations, such as Shanghai Cooperation Organisation Energy Club,[8] multilateral platforms with Africa,[9] and joint initiation for clean technology cooperation.[10] This evolution

---

2. Atanu Ghoshray and Javier Ordóñez, 'The Chinese Energy-Intensive Growth Model and Its Impact on Commodity Markets', in *Energy Security and Sustainable Economic Growth in China*, ed. Shujie Yao and Maria Jesus Herrerias Herrera's (London: Palgrave Macmillan, 2014), 31–51.
3. For example, China's oil and gas pipeline with Central Asian countries and Russia. See Susann Handke, *Securing and Fuelling China's Ascent to Power: The Geopolitics of the Chinese-Kazakh Oil Pipeline* (Hague: Clingendael International Energy Programme, 2006), http://www.clingendaelenergy.com/inc/upload/files/Chinese-Kazakh_Oil_Pipeline.pdf; Keunwook Paik, 'Sino-Russian Gas and Oil Cooperation: Entering into a New Era of Strategic Partnership?', Oxford Institute for Energy Studies, 2015, https://www.oxfordenergy.org/wpcms/wp-content/uploads/2015/04/WPM-59.pdf.
4. Ivana Casaburi, 'Chinese Investment in Europe', ESADE China Europe Club, 2016, http://itemsweb.esade.edu/research/esadegeo/ENGChineseInvestmentInEurope201516.pdf; Jeremy Clegg and Hinrich Voss, 'Chinese Overseas Direct Investment in the European Union', in *China and the EU in Context*, ed. Kerry Brown (London: Palgrave Macmillan, 2014), 14–43.
5. James Kynge, 'Western Resistance to China Blocks $40bn of Acquisitions', *Financial Times*, 25 October 2016.
6. See Chapter 2.
7. See Chapter 1.
8. See Chapter 3.
9. See Chapter 4.
10. See Chapter 5.

in China's energy policy, from energy diplomacy to a strategy that incorporates global energy governance, has raised the question about the extent to which China would work with multilateralism.

A Debate of Chinese Energy Security

Energy has been linked with diplomacy and security throughout human history, and continues to be a core aspect in business and politics. In the early twentieth century, competition for oil in the Persian Gulf triggered the British-Russian conflict. The Italian invasion of Abyssinia in 1935[11] and the German invasion of the Soviet Union in 1941[12] were also linked to the desire for oil. Diplomatic approaches to energy are frequently adopted in modern international relations. For instance, the US has been investing in extensive diplomatic efforts to ensure global oil supplies. Washington has attempted to 'promote a stable global energy supply by engaging diplomatic partners and private producers to maintain supply, calm markets, and pursue alternative energy options'.[13] In the new millennium, tightening global oil and gas markets and new energy abundance has upended global politics, attracting academic attention towards how energy is shaping foreign affairs. [14]

Energy has also been a key agenda in global governance. The governance of energy issues beyond the national level is regarded as global energy governance, and this relies on a multilateral approach at both global and regional levels.[15] Since the late 1970s, the liberalisation of the international energy market, particularly the oil market, has marked a starting point for a paradigm of global energy governance. In simpler words, the oil shocks of the 1970s fundamentally changed the rules of the game in the international energy market. This is well demonstrated by the formation of the International Energy

---

11. Cristiano Andrea Ristuccia, '1935 Sanctions Against Italy: Would Coal and Crude Oil Have Made a Difference', *European Review of Economic History* 4, no. 1 (2000): 85–110.
12. Keith Crane, *Imported Oil and US National Security* (Washington: RAND Corporation, 2009).
13. US DOS, 'Energy Diplomacy in the 21st Century', 2012, http://www.state.gov/r/pa/pl/2012/200637.htm.
14. Meghan O'Sullivan, Windfall: How the new energy abundance upends global politics and strengthens America's power (New York: Simon & Schuster, 2017).
15. See Andrew Goldthau, 'Governing Global Energy: Existing Approaches and Discourses', *Current Opinion in Environmental Sustainability* 3, no. 4 (2011): 213–217; for other studies on global energy governance, see Aleh Cherp, Jessica Jewell, and Andrew Goldthau, 'Governing Global Energy: Systems, Transitions, Complexity', *Global Policy* 2, no. 1 (2011): 75–88; Gaye Christoffersen, 'The Dilemmas of China's Energy Governance: Recentralization and Regional Cooperation', *The China and Eurasia Form Quarterly* 3, no. 3 (2005): 55–80; Navroz K. Dubash and Ann Florini, 'Mapping Global Energy Governance', *Global Policy* 2, no. 1 (2011): 6–18; Ann Florini, 'The International Energy Agency in Global Energy Governance', *Global Policy* 2, no. 1 (2011): 40–50; Arunabha Ghosh, 'Seeking Coherence in Complexity? The Governance of Energy by Trade and Investment Institutions', *Global Policy* 2, no. 1 (2011): 106–119; Maria van der Hoeven, 'IEA Vision on International Energy Governance', *Energy Strategy Reviews* 1, no. 2 (2012): 73–75.

Agency (IEA). In the 1970s, oil-importing countries experienced tremendous difficulties in replacing oil supplies that were lost due to the oil embargo and the associated political turmoil in the Persian Gulf. Thus, the consumer countries of the Organization of Economic Cooperation and Development (OECD) created emergency sharing mechanisms and combined forces via the IEA. Since then, several energy-related international and regional institutions have been established, such as the Energy Charter, the IRENA, the IEF, and the energy working group under the G20. A multilateral approach is followed to deal with energy issues in the form of institutions that constitute formal rules, informal constraints, and enforcement mechanisms. Global energy governance is being established, developed, and advanced as a new and promising approach that relies on governments' commitment to the paradigm of global energy governance.[16]

To enhance energy security, China has adopted energy diplomacy as an important part of its 'going-out' strategy and national development strategy.[17] Zhu argues that energy diplomacy is a logical extension of China's national interests, as it builds relations with resource-rich countries, develops a favourable environment for Chinese companies in the resource field, and establishes alliances for energy cooperation.[18] For China, the primary goal of energy diplomacy is to secure national control of overseas resource supplies, particularly oil and gas, and to diversify its import sources. Moreover, since the sustainable development of the Chinese economy is closely related to the sustainable development of the world economy, the world has started to keep an eye on China's actions.

China's energy hunt was not always well accepted by the international community. It is generally understood that energy import-dependent states tend to expand their influence in the global market by increasing relative and absolute power, and China is no exception.[19] Since energy 'could be a catalyst for conflict',[20] China's energy security strategy could lead to the insecurity of other countries.[21] Some even view China's expanding international

---

16. Goldthau, 'Governing Global Energy: Existing Approaches and Discourses', 213–217.
17. PRC State Council, 'An Overview of "Going Out" Strategy', 2011, http://qwgzyj.gqb.gov.cn/yjytt/159/1743.shtml; Qinhua Xu, 'China's Energy Diplomacy and its Implications for Global Energy Security', FES Briefing Paper, 2007, http://library.fes.de/pdf-files/iez/global/04763.pdf.
18. Feng Zhu, 'A High Price to Pay: China's Resource Diplomacy Requires Wisdom', *New Finance*, 18 May 2005, accessed 13 September 2013, http://media.163.com/05/0518/10/1K1FC60A00141A16.html.
19. See also Chietigj Bajpaee, 'China Fuels Energy Cold War', *Asia Times*, 2 March 2005, http://www.atimes.com/atimes/China/GC02Ad07.html; Steven Mufson, 'As China, U.S. Vie for More Oil, Diplomatic Friction May Follow', *Washington Post*, 15 April 2006, http://www.washingtonpost.com/wp-dyn/content/article/2006/04/14/AR2006041401682_2.html.
20. Kent Calder, *Pacific Defense: Arms, Energy, and America's Future in Asia* (New York: William Morrow & Co., 2006).
21. Daivd Zweig and Mikkal Herberg, 'China's Energy Rise, the US, and the New Geopolitics of Energy', *Pacific Council on International Policy* (2010): 35–74; David Zweig, 'A New

cooperation as a way to step up control of the global energy supply chain for its own benefit.[22] The US, in a national report, suggested that China could somehow 'lock up' energy supplies or seek to direct markets and support resource-rich countries without regard to their political stance.[23] For example, in 2020, amid trade tensions and disruptions due to the COVID-19 pandemic, Chinese President Xi called for the need to diversify imports and strengthen the global supply chain's dependence on China. The underlying rationale was to 'develop power retaliation and deterrence capabilities against supply cut-offs by foreign parties'.[24] The China-Australia dispute over coal trade in 2020–2021 was another example of a resource commodity used as geopolitical leverage during diplomatic disputes.

However, others have also indicated that the impact of China's vast investment could be an opportunity to enhance cooperation and interdependence rather than as a threat.[25] Indeed, Chinese energy companies have explored energy reserves in regions where no Western powers can or will invest. Such an approach increases the world's available energy reserves, and hence, instead of harming global energy security, China's energy policy actually enhances it.[26] Moreover, beyond bilateral energy diplomacy, China has also proactively participated in international energy organisations and advocated global governance as a means to handle global energy issues, from market disruption to low-carbon transition.

Despite its lack of confidence in Western-led institutions and traditional preference for bilateral diplomatic approaches, China has repeatedly pledged to participate actively in global energy and climate governance in recent years. China's white paper on energy in 2007 first emphasised the country's contribution to international energy cooperation via both bilateral and multilateral approaches.[27] The energy white papers in 2012 and 2020 further addressed the need for global energy governance in stabilising the global market. The action

---

"Trading State" Meets the Developing World', Working Paper no. 31, Center on China's Transnational Relations of the Hong Kong University of Science and Technology; David Zweig and Bi Jianhai, 'China's Global Hunt for Energy', *Foreign Affairs* 8, no. 5 (2005): 25–38.

22. Jean Garrison, *China and the Energy Equation in Asia: The Determinants of Policy Choice* (Boulder, CO: Lynne Rienner Publishers, 2009); Dobie Langenkamp, 'Our Friend, The Dragon', *Energy Tribune*, 2010, http://www.energytribune.com/articles.cfm?aid=3758.
23. White House, 'The National Security Strategy', 2006, https://www.comw.org/qdr/fulltext/nss2006.pdf.
24. Jinping Xi, '国家中长期经济社会发展战略若干重大问题' [Major issues in the National medium- to long-term economic and social development strategy], *Qiushi*, 31 October 2020, http://www.xinhuanet.com/politics/leaders/2020-10/31/c_1126681658.htm.
25. Philip Andrews-Speed, *The Strategic Implications of China's Energy Needs* (London: Routledge, 2014).
26. US DOE, 'Energy Policy Act of 2005 Section 1837: National Security Review of International Energy Requirements', 2006, https://www.govinfo.gov/content/pkg/PLAW-109publ58/pdf/PLAW-109publ58.pdf.
27. PRC NDRC, 'China's Energy Conditions and Policies', 2007, https://en.ndrc.gov.cn/policies/202105/P020210527780237298276.pdf.

plan for carbon dioxide reduction in 2021 highlighted global governance as an important way to achieve energy transition. Global energy governance is also incorporated into China's grand strategy—the Belt and Road Initiative. China's top leadership has repeatedly called for a global effort to tackle energy problems collectively and proposed the establishment of an international institute to govern the energy market.[28]

While China's rise in global governance is widely seen as part of the solution to global energy and climate challenges, there has also been a long debate whether China's strategy seeks to work within the multilateral system as a 'responsible stakeholder' or outside the system via its preferred approaches. While China has been actively expanding its footprint in international energy cooperation and international energy organisations, it remains unclear how China would fit into the existing global energy governance system.

Structure of the Subsequent Chapters

This book attempts to unpack the rationale, mechanism, and evolution underpinning China's strategy for international energy cooperation in the following chapters. Chapter 1 begins by discussing the historical background, structure, policy priority, and rationale behind China's energy security from the late 1990s to 2021.[29] It outlines and explores how Chinese energy diplomacy has evolved to adopt a more balanced approach that incorporates global governance for addressing energy and climate challenges.

Chapter 2 attempts to unpack the key aspects of energy cooperation in the BRI. It also uses the case of the Asia Infrastructure Investment Bank (AIIB) to explain how global energy governance is implemented. The chapter provides a deep dive into China's view towards international energy organisations. It also analyses whether BRI is turning China's energy cooperation in Eurasia into more of a multilateral strategy.

Chapter 3 offers a case study of China's pipeline projects in Central Asia. Specifically, it looks at the development of cross-border oil and gas pipelines and the attitude of relevant parties towards multilateral organisations, such as the Shanghai Cooperation Organization, which can facilitate energy trade via transnational pipelines. This chapter seeks to determine whether China's energy strategy in Central Asia has taken a more multilateral approach, especially in the area of infrastructure connectivity.

Chapter 4 turns to Africa and looks at Chinese oil and gas investment in the continent. It analyses the mechanisms China uses to enhance its cooperation

---

28. UPI, 'China Urges Global Energy Cooperation', *United Press International*, 16 January 2021, http://www.upi.com/Business_News/Energy-Resources/2012/01/16/China-urges-global-energy-cooperation/UPI-77361326740422.
29. This research does not cover the Russia-Ukraine crisis that broke out in March 2022.

with African countries, from diplomatic means to high-level events such as the Forum of Africa-China Cooperation. This chapter uncovers whether China's energy strategy in Africa is able to show a multilateral approach or merely rely on bilateral approaches.

Chapter 5 presents a third case study on the EU-China clean energy cooperation. The energy relationship between China and the EU is explored, focusing on technology transfer and joint projects/initiatives that promote low-carbon development. It explains how international commitment to climate change, such as the Paris Agreement, has driven cooperation and the key obstacles in this context.

The final chapter offers a conclusion. It summarises the findings in the above case studies and discusses the extent to which China's energy strategy has incorporated global energy governance. It analyses the key challenges as well as the geopolitical consequences of China utilising global governance to deal with energy and climate issues across the Eurasian region.

1
Evolution of Chinese Energy and Climate Strategy

From Going-Out Strategy to the Belt and Road Initiative

China's energy security has evolved over time from a traditional 'self-reliance' approach of securing supply for economic and geopolitical goals to a more balanced strategy that incorporates solutions for emerging challenges, such as carbon neutrality[1] and social instability.[2] The current energy challenges that China faces do not primarily entail domestic production and resource trade, but are also in the diversification of sources and transportation routes as well as in the structural contradictions arising from the need for balance between economic growth and sustainable development. Over the last few decades, these challenges have been intensified by a series of risks, such as financial crises, oil price fluctuations, trade wars, the COVID-19 pandemic, social instability and extreme weather events. How Chinese authorities address these issues was reflected in the evolution of Chinese energy security.

Scholars study energy security through different dimensions and interdisciplinarity, including geopolitics, economy, and science. In this thesis, energy security refers to 'the availability of energy at all times in various forms, in sufficient quantities, and at affordable prices'.[3] The actual practice of energy security strategies inevitably relies on international cooperation, which can be in the form of energy diplomacy (a bilateral approach) and/or global energy governance (a multilateral approach).

1. For China's climate challenges, see Henry Lee, Daniel Schrag, Matthew Bunn, Michael Davidson, Wei Peng, Wang Pu, and Mao Zhimin, *Foundations for a Low-Carbon Energy System in China* (Cambridge: Cambridge University Press, 2021).
2. Social instability created by a lack of energy supply.
3. UNDP, 'World Energy Assessment: Energy and the Challenge of Sustainability', 2000, https://www.undp.org/sites/g/files/zskgke326/files/publications/World%20Energy%20Assessment-2000.pdf. See also Janusz Bielecki, 'Energy Security: Is the Wolf at the Door?' *The Quarterly Review of Economics and Finance* 42, no. 2 (2002): 235–250; Danial Yergin, 'Energy Security in the 1990s', *Foreign Affairs* 67, no. 1 (1988): 110–132; IEA, *World Energy Outlook 2007: China and India insights* (Paris: OECD, 2007); Robert B. Krueger, *The United States and International Oil* (New York: Praeger Publisher, 1975).

A Historical Overview of China's Energy Security and Strategy

From 1949 to 1992: The mentality of self-reliance

Traditionally, the concept of Chinese energy security has featured highly strategic, economic, and geopolitical considerations.[4] Impelled by the objective of every country to survive and progress, energy production has became the focus of competition in the world, especially in China, whose energy demand increased rapidly following the opening up of the country's economy in the 1980s. China needs a stable and sufficient supply of energy to support rapid economic development, socio-political stability, and sovereignty.[5] In summary, the concept of self-sufficiency (or self-reliance) underpins China's energy security.[6]

When China was established, its external oil dependence rate was very high because the oil industry was in recovery and going through an exploratory stage.[7] Therefore, Chinese energy security was historically equated to oil security owing to China's increasing reliance on foreign oil and the desire for self-sufficiency. As a critical fuel for the economic engine, oil is equivalent to Chinese security. In the 1950s and 1960s, when China relied heavily on imported oil, the US oil trade embargo and the termination of the Soviet oil supply left Chinese leaders in a desperate state, which continued to be a painful memory. They learned an important lesson: the supply of imported oil is not always reliable and can easily be interrupted by hostile parties for

---

4. See Philip Andrews-Speed, *Energy Policy and Regulation in the People's Republic of China* (London: Kluwer Law International, 2004).
5. In order to maintain its authority, the CPC needs to meet people's economic and nationalistic expectations. As Breslin argues, 'it is an unwritten social contract between the party and the people whereby the people do not compete with the party for political power as long as the party looks after their economic fortunes.' See Shaun Breslin, 'Power and Production: Rethinking China's Global Economic Role', *Review of International Studies* 31, no. 4 (2005): 735–753.
6. Guy Leung, 'China's Energy Security: Perception and Reality', *Energy Policy* 39, no. 3 (2011): 1330–1337.
7. Since the foundation of the PRC, coal has been the major energy source consumed, and occupies almost 70% of China's energy mix nowadays. Chinese authorities pay less attention to coal in China's energy security because the country has abundant coal reserves, but the situation is different in relation to oil. Moreover, currently, coal and oil are used in different sectors: power generation and transportation, respectively. Since the Westernisation Movement (1861–1894) in the late Qing dynasty (1644–1977), coal has been the main energy source in China's energy consumption structure. This only started to change from the 1960s. So far, the proportion of coal in China's energy consumption structure still fluctuates around 70%, while oil only accounts for about 20%, so China is still in the coal era. Due to concerns about energy security, China adopted a negative attitude towards its energy structure, which is actually against the trend to optimise the use of energy. Before the '11th Five Year Plan', China continued to emphasise a 'coal-based' energy structure due to coal's fundamental and strategic position; after the 'Eleventh Five-Year Plan', as a result of pressure due to climate change, China has not mentioned the 'coal basis', but will likely maintain a 'coal-based' energy structure for the foreseeable future.

geopolitical reasons. The breakdown in China–Soviet Union relations further drove China to adopt a comprehensive self-sufficiency policy and formulate an energy security strategy.

The discovery of the Daqing and Shengli oil fields in 1959 and 1962 marked a new phase for China's oil industry. In the subsequent years, the development of more oil fields, such as Huabei, Dagang, Liaohe, Changqing, Henan, Zhongyuan, and Jianghan, boosted China's oil production and made the country self-sufficient in oil in 1963.[8] A rapid rise in oil production fundamentally eased tensions arising from energy supply issues and changed the backward situation of China's oil industry. After 1973, China began to export crude oil to Japan, Thailand, the Philippines, Romania, etc. However, it soon witnessed a decrease in oil exports caused by the slowing down of oil production and the increasing demand for oil as a result of rapid domestic economic development.

From 1993 to 2002: The supply-oriented agenda

In 1993, China turned from a net oil exporter into a net oil importer,[9] driving authorities to prioritise supply security and, in turn, encourage Chinese energy companies to go overseas as part of the 'going out' strategy. In the 1990s, China's economy developed rapidly due to its reforms and opening up. China had to rely on imported oil because its domestic oil production failed to meet its demand. The external dependence continued to increase as per the annual increase in import volume. In 1999, China's dependence on foreign oil increased to over 20%.[10] This marked the moment of China adjusting its energy policy to prioritise securing overseas supply alongside its long-term goal to achieve self-sufficiency.

The security of imported oil became a more pressing issue, especially in the domestic economy and geopolitical competitions. China once attempted to boost the domestic production of existing oil fields, develop new and offshore oil fields, increase oil consumption efficiency, and impose temporary oil import bans. However, since none of the above measures could reverse the growing dependence on foreign oil, China continued to import it. As a result, supply security remained the core objective of China's energy policy over the next few decades.

With this background, China put forward a goal for energy security, which was to 'ensure a stable long-term oil supply'.[11] Consequently, Chinese national oil companies started to go overseas for energy resources. Their overseas

---

8. Daojiong Zha, 中国石油安全的国际政治经济学分析 [Analysis of the international political economy of China's oil security] (Beijing: Contemporary World Publisher, 2005).
9. PRC NBS, *China Energy Statistical Yearbook 2013* (Beijing: China Statistics Press, 2013).
10. Ibid.
11. Felix K Chang 'Chinese Energy and Asian Security', *Orbis* 145, no. 2 (2001): 211–240.

activities covered pipeline construction, oil and gas exploration, ground infrastructure, the petrochemical industry, petroleum refining, petroleum sales, etc.[12] Increased FDI allowed Chinese energy companies to familiarise themselves with the international energy investment environment and obtain useful experience for further M&A. In 1998, China reformed its price formation mechanism of oil products, establishing a connection between domestic oil and international oil prices. This move marked the beginning of the internationalisation of China's oil production.[13]

Around the end of the twentieth century, in order to secure its growth rate and reduce import dependency, China introduced the 'going out' strategy to encourage more Chinese investment overseas. Under this strategy, Chinese oil companies took the initiative to develop overseas energy and natural resources operations that expand their footprint globally over the next two decades.

From 2002 to 2012: Going-out strategy in the context of climate change

In the 2000s, a two-fold need for overseas energy investment and sustainable development reshaped China's energy security. China faced growing geopolitical tensions and climate issues and had to accommodate these in its energy strategy. Meanwhile, its dependency on imported oil continued to increase due to the rapid rise in oil demand in the transportation sector and across various industries.[14] As a solution, China adopted an 'open source and reduce expenditure' approach. While 'open source' referred to increasing supply options, particularly via more overseas investment under the 'going out' strategy, 'reduce expenditure' was designed to address domestic environmental problems. This concept directed how China developed its energy security in the 11th Five Year Plan[15] and was further embodied by official development plans.

China's global hunt for oil fuelled the so-called 'China energy threat' discourse have complicated the global environment in which China has been trying to secure its energy supply.[16] There was growing concern that Western

---

12. Zha, 'Analysis of the International Political Economy of China's Oil Security'.
13. Dan Shi, '我国能源政策回顾与未来的政策' ['China's energy policy and future policy review'], *Economic Research Reference* 20 (2000): 20–27.
14. Bi Fan, *The New World Energy Order: The Impact of US 'Energy Independence' and China's Response* (Beijing: China Economy Publisher, 2014).
15. Gaye Christoffersen, 'The Dilemmas of China's Energy Governance: Recentralization and Regional Cooperation', *The China and Eurasia Form Quarterly* 3, no. 3 (2005): 64; Christian Constantin, 'China's Conception of Energy Security: Sources and International Impacts' (Working Paper no. 43, the University of British Columbia, 2005), https://sppga.ubc.ca/news/chinas-conception-of-energy-security-sources-and-international-impacts/.
16. David Zweig, 'A New "Trading State" Meets the Developing World', Working Paper no. 31, Center on China's Transnational Relations of the Hong Kong University of Science and Technology; David Zweig and Bi Jianhai, 'China's Global Hunt for Energy', *Foreign Affairs*

governments would impose strict regulations on Chinese overseas energy and resource investment based on national security. For instance, the Chinese oil company CNOOC had to drop its bid to buy US oil firm Union Oil Company of California (UNOCAL) in 2005 since the US considered such a deal to be a national security threat and violation of fair trade.[17] Similarly, in the face of increasing foreign direct investment (FDI) from China, both Canada and Australia imposed strict measures on state-owned energy investments in their recent investment guidelines.[18] China's association with the World Trade Organization (WTO) in 2001 also meant that it had to deal with not only its oil importers, but also the regional and global oil markets.

Another emerging security concern was the safety of maritime traffic. Some scholars have expounded that the increasingly saturated carrying capacity of the Malacca Strait has exposed China's energy security to significant risks, from piracy and terrorist attacks to sealine disruption by hostile countries. Therefore, the 'Malacca dilemma' represents an issue of economic, geopolitical, and military security. In 2003, President Hu Jintao publicly claimed that 'certain powers' were attempting to control the Malacca Strait, through which over 80% of the imported oil travels to China, and hence threatening the security of China's oil supply.[19]

In response, China attempted to speed up expanding its supply options by encouraging its energy companies to invest overseas as part of the broader 'going-out' strategy. According to Zhang Guobao, former Director of NEA, Chinese energy companies signed 131 contracts with 43 countries and regions on oil and gas exploration and refining, pipeline construction, and technological service during the 11th Five Year Plan period.[20] The scope of cooperation was expanded from oil and gas to coal, electric power, and clean energy. By late 2009, Chinese energy companies' overseas oil production reached 50 million tonnes, raising the country's security level of overseas energy sources.[21] Among them, the Central Asia–China gas pipeline and the Myanmar-China oil and gas pipeline are flagship projects that demonstrate China's ambition to enhance energy security via overseas investment. In the wake of the economic crisis in 2009, Chinese energy companies took advantage of the decreasing international energy demand and dropping energy prices to improve their domestic industry, strengthen international energy cooperation,

---

8, no. 5 (2005): 25–38; Daivd Zweig and Mikkal Herberg, 'China's Energy Rise, the US, and the New Geopolitics of Energy', *Pacific Council on International Policy*, (2010): 35–74.
17. Matt Pottinger, 'CNOOC Drops Offer for Unocal, Exposing U.S.-Chinese Tensions', *Wall Street Journal*, 3 August 2005, https://www.wsj.com/articles/SB112295744495102393.
18. Jeff Lewis and Melanie Burton, 'Chinese Miners' Deal Frenzy Seen Stalling on Regulatory Hurdles', *Reuters*, 6 July 2020.
19. Marc Lanteigne, 'China's Maritime Security and the "Malacca Dilemma"', *Asian Security* 4, no. 2 (2008): 143–161.
20. Guobao Zhang, Speech in The Observer Forum 2010, Beijing, 1 January 2011.
21. PRC NEA, 2009年能源经济形势及2010年展望 [2009 energy economic situation and prospects 2010] (Beijing: NEA, 2010).

and establish a secure, stable, and clean energy supply system. These efforts helped maintain the stable development of the energy industry and support the fast-developing national economy.

Chinese authorities had not only attempted to strengthen its supply security, but also actively explored ways to enhance environmental protection, which was undermined by rapid economic development. In October 2003, China introduced the Scientific Outlook on Development, which emphasised a harmonious balance between the development of society and nature.[22] Later in 2014, China passed the Outline of China's Medium and Long-Term Energy Development Plan in the State Council's executive meeting.[23] The principles for energy development put forth in the outline were as follows: 'Energy saving is the priority while efficiency is the basis; coal is the basis while diversification of energy is encouraged; domestic market is the foothold while the overseas market is to be explored; urban and rural areas should be planned as a whole and the layout should be appropriate; technology is to be depended on and institutional innovation is needed; the environment should be protected while security should be ensured.'[24]

In 2006, China's Five-Year Plan continued to reinforce the country's climate focus, such as enhancing resource-strengthening environmental protection, conservation in economic development, improving resource utilisation efficiency, and curbing ecological and environmental degradation.[25] According to the government, China was set to make resource saving a priority and establish a stable, economical, clean, and secure energy supply system. The ultimate goal was to build a resource-saving and environmentally friendly society.[26] In 2007, the National Development and Reform Commission (NDRC) formulated the 11th Five Year Plan for Energy Development[27] and outlined the Scientific Outlook on Development and Construction of a Harmonious Socialist Society as the two guiding principles for energy development, and it put effort into establishing a stable, economic, and clean energy system to support sustainable social and economic development along with sustainable development of energy.[28] Despite the lack of a detailed action plan, these high-level policies demonstrated that China started to incorporate sustainable development and climate issues in its energy strategy alongside overseas energy investment.

---

22. Xinhua News, 'Scientific Outlook on Development', *China Daily*, 8 September 2010.
23. Xinhua News, '国务院常务会议原则通过《能源中长期发展规划纲要》' ['Energy and Long-Term Development Plan' approved in State Council executive meeting]', *Xinhua News*, 1 July 2004, http://news.xinhuanet.com/zhengfu/2004-07/01/content_1559228.htm.
24. Ibid.
25. PRC State Council, 'The 11th Five-Year Plan', PRC State Council, 2006, http://www.gov.cn/gongbao/content/2006/content_268766.htm.
26. Ibid.
27. PRC NDRC, '能源发展"十一五"规划' [Energy development 'Eleventh Five-Year' Plan]', 2007, http://zfxxgk.nea.gov.cn/auto79/201109/P020110921527315023013.pdf.
28. Ibid.

From 2013 to 2021: Belt and Road, carbon neutrality, and self-sufficiency[29]

Since Xi Jinping took office as the president of China, energy security has undergone rapid progression. This has been driven by multiple factors, including the BRI, the Paris Agreement, and supply chain disruptions due to the trade war and COVID-19 pandemic. These major issues and crises have reshaped China's energy strategy with emerging elements, such as global governance, energy transition, and supply chain control. Unlike its previous approach to energy security, acquiring energy resources abroad is not the primary or sole objective of energy cooperation. Instead, China's strategic focus has shifted from quantitative objectives (e.g., increasing the amount of imported oil) to qualitative objectives (e.g., upgrading supply chain and sustainable development).[30]

China launched the Belt and Road Initiative in 2013.[31] As an upgraded version of the 'going-out' strategy, the BRI is an ambitious development project with strong geopolitical and economic dimensions that intends to revive and modernise the historic Silk Road cooperation. Energy is a key aspect of the BRI, as reflected in the official document of the initiative.[32] Energy cooperation in the BRI focuses not only on imports of resources, but also on industry development, policy coordination, energy finance, sustainable development, and governance structure. Transnational energy cooperation, especially the massive development of energy infrastructure and improved market access, is an important means for China to achieve its ambitious goals. Under the BRI, China signed a number of flagship energy agreements, including the Russia-China gas pipeline (Eastern route) in 2014, the Yamal LNG deal in 2017, and Artic LNG 2 in 2019.

BRI energy cooperation is expected to support China in addressing a number of challenges, including China's economic transformation, exploration of new markets, managing domestic excess capacity and production, as well as regional security and the growing negativity of neighbouring countries.[33] Beyond these factors, overseas investment built on energy infrastructures and

---

29. This research does not cover the Russia-Ukraine crisis that broke out in March 2022.
30. A former Chinese oil company researcher, interview with the author, 2014.
31. See Chapter 2.
32. PRC NEA, 'Vision and Actions on Energy Cooperation in Jointly Building Silk Road Economic Belt and 21st-Century Maritime Silk Road', PRC NEA, 2017, http://www.nea.gov.cn/2017-05/12/c_136277478.htm.
33. Pepe Escobar, 'The Eurasian Big Bang: How China and Russia Are Carving Out Their Own World Order', *Energy Post*, 25 August 2015; Lucy Hornby, 2016, 'China seeks foreign investors for One Belt, One Road push', *Financial Times*, 25 May 2016; Dragan Pavlićević, 2015. 'China, the EU and One Belt, One Road strategy', *China Brief* 15, no. 15 (2015), http://www.jamestown.org/programs/chinabrief/single/?tx_ttnews%5Btt_news%5D=44235&cHash=9dbc08472c19ecd691307c4c1905eb0c#.V9-58CTuCXs.

trade would allow China to bolster and solidify its geopolitical standing.[34] The Chinese government emphasised that strengthening energy cooperation by jointly building the BRI can 'stimulate wider and deeper regional cooperation at a higher level for the economic prosperity of the whole world'.[35] In terms of connectivity, energy cooperation in the BRI is expected to be an integrated and multilateral engagement strategy.

Signing the Paris Agreement in 2016 has redefined Chinese energy security and energy cooperation with more robust climate agendas. While Chinese authorities sought to accommodate climate finance and sustainable development under the BRI framework, it also introduced a nationwide carbon market. China pledged to strictly control the emission of pollutants and greenhouse gases, raise energy efficiency, and contribute to green and efficient development in both domestic and overseas projects. This statement implied that certain environmental conditions would be included in the BRI's energy investments.

China continued to step up its climate effort in 2020 despite the pandemic disruption. During a UN General Assembly meeting, President Xi outlined China's aspiration to hit peak emissions before 2030 and become carbon neutral before 2060. A year later, China released a new decarbonisation framework—Action Plan for Carbon Dioxide Peaking Before 2030, restating the country's goals for 2025 and 2030.[36] Such declarations are an affirmation of China's ambition to transition towards low-carbon development in its overall energy strategy. In his speech at the UN General Assembly on 21 September 2021, President Xi pledged that China would not build new coal-fired power plants overseas and would step up support for other emerging nations in developing green and low-carbon energy.[37]

During COP26 Glasgow in November 2021, China called on developed countries to provide support to help developing countries do better in dealing with the climate crisis.[38] It also submitted an updated National Determined Contribution (NDC) to the United Nations with slightly more ambitious targets than previously, reaffirming Beijing's pledge to peak carbon emissions before 2030. However, its last-minute intervention together with India to weaken the language on fossil fuel in the Glasgow Climate Pact reflected that the Chinese government would only adopt a conservative plan for energy

---

34. George Magnus, 'China Must Prove Silk Road Plan Is Serious', *Financial Times*, 4 May 2015.
35. PRC NDRC, PRC MFA, and PRC MOFCOM, 'Vision and Actions on Jointly Building the Silk Road Economic Belt and the 21st-Century Maritime Silk Road', PRC NDRC, 2015, https://www.fmprc.gov.cn/eng/topics_665678/2015zt/xjpcxbayzlt2015nnh/201503/t20150328_705553.html.
36. PRC NDRC, 'Action Plan for Carbon Dioxide China', PRC NDRC, 2021, https://en.ndrc.gov.cn/policies/202110/t20211027_1301020.html.
37. UN, 'China Headed towards Carbon Neutrality by 2060; President Xi Jinping Vows to Halt New Coal Plants Abroad', United Nations, 2021.
38. E3G, 'China's New NDC—E3G Responds', E3G, 2022, https://www.e3g.org/news/china-s-new-ndc-e3g-responds/.

transition with a limited negative impact on its economy. These all put China under the spotlight over whether it would be able to ensure domestic growth and advance decarbonisation in other developing countries amid international pressure for more emissions reduction.

New energy policies and emerging environmental focus does not mean that China has departed from its traditional understanding of energy security. In April 2020, in response to the COVID-19 pandemic and trade war, President Xi repeatedly highlighted energy security in government meetings and speeches. In late April, the NEA issued a list of policy areas that it would focus on in 2020, including power supply, grid networks, oil and gas infrastructure, and coal projects. The statement issued reflected that due to supply chain disruptions during the pandemic and trade war, China had to prioritise the security of critical supply for growth and social stability, bringing back its initial outlook of self-reliance. Power shortage driven by aggressive coal consumption cap later in the year highlighted the importance of ensuring basic energy security to avoid social instability.[39] Indeed, even China's action plan for carbon reduction in 2021 reaffirmed that traditional energy security was the bottom line of the country.

China's energy white paper—Energy in China's New Era in 2020—adequately summarised China's energy and climate strategy for the decade. The white paper introduced a new energy security strategy centred around a conservative approach towards balancing environmental goals and development needs, achieving greater self-reliance, and creating a clean and diversified energy supply system. On the one hand, it confirmed China's target of achieving carbon neutrality by 2060 and reiterated strong policy support for renewable energy. On the other, in pursuit of greater self-reliance, the strategy promoted domestic fossil fuel production and considered cleaner and more efficient utilisation of fossil fuels as part of China's 'green development'. It also indicated that non-fossil fuels, particularly renewable and nuclear energy, would play an increasingly crucial role in China's energy mix supply system despite their current modest contribution.

Beijing's revisit of the 'self-reliance' priority in this policy period reflects China's dilemma of energy transition. Despite increasing climate pressure from the international community, it has proven to be unrealistic for China to remove fossil fuels altogether, especially coal, oil, and gas, from its energy structure over the next decade. A key driver behind Beijing's bid to bolster energy security is its heavy dependence on energy imports, which represents a strategic vulnerability in a world characterised by rising geopolitical rivalries. In short, Beijing wants to boost domestic fossil fuel production in pursuit of 'self-reliance' while simultaneously pursuing a gradual energy transition.

---

39. Phipip Andrews-Speed, 'China's Energy Crisis: Unstoppable Force Meets Immoveable Object'. Philip Andrews-Speed personal page. http://www.andrewsspeed.com/chinas-energy-crisis-unstoppable-force-meets-immoveable-object/.

Chinese Energy Strategy: From Energy Diplomacy to Global Energy Governance?

China's quest for energy security traditionally involved a combination of strategic, economic, and geopolitical considerations. According to the IEA's study on 'China's Worldwide Quest for Energy Security', there are five 'basic strategies' to ensure energy security: 'developing domestic resources to the maximum possible, creating strategic reserves, seeking foreign technology and investment, establishing reliable and secure oil trading channels, and making strategic investments in upstream production facilities abroad.'[40] These strategies rely on various forms of coordination in international cooperation that can be broadly categorised under energy diplomacy and global energy governance.

The literature on Chinese external energy security policy defines energy diplomacy as government-involved foreign activities that aim to secure an energy resource supply and promote energy business cooperation.[41] Due to the unique nature of the energy market, China's international energy cooperation has hitherto relied heavily on country-to-country deals. Energy diplomacy is often carried out bilaterally and requires policy coordination between the two countries concerned. Hence, energy diplomacy 'differentiates relations case-by-case based principally on a priori particularistic grounds or situational exigencies'.[42] In sum, energy diplomacy is a bilateral way of coordinating energy policy that includes diplomatic relations, economic agreements, and FDI between two countries.

In contrast to the bilateral approach of energy diplomacy, global energy governance is characterised by multilateralisation and institutionalisation. Global energy governance has been defined as the application 'of all multilateral regulations intended for [the] organization and centralization of global energy activities' and 'the setting and enforcement of rules and regulations for global collective energy interests'.[43] It is underpinned by the logic that global institutions are required for the creation of global public goods. Challenges to cross-border energy governance and market failures that require government intervention at the global level can come in various forms, from energy price

---

40. IEA, *China's Worldwide Quest for Energy Security* (Paris: IEA, 2000), 74.
41. See Shaofeng Chen, 'Motivations behind China's Foreign Oil Quest: A Perspective from the Chinese Government and the Oil Companies', *Journal of Chinese Political Science* 13, no. 1 (2008): 79–104; Ian Taylor 'China's Oil Diplomacy in Africa', *International Affairs* 82, no. 5 (2006): 937–959; Amy Myers Jaffe and Steven Lewis, 'Beijing's Oil Diplomacy', *Survival* 44, no. 1 (2002): 115–134.
42. John Ruggie, 'Multilateralism: The Anatomy of an Institution', *International Organization* 46, no. 3 (1992): 561–598.
43. Bo Kong, 'Governing China's Energy in the Context of Global Governance', *Global Policy* 2, no. 1 (2011): 51–65.

stabilisation[44] to climate change.[45] Global energy governance relies on multilateral cooperation at both the global and regional levels.

Examining China's approach to multilateralism can help indicate whether its energy strategy is moving towards global energy governance or remains governed by energy diplomacy. The importance of multilateralism in global energy governance may be understood via the connection between multilateralism and global governance. Global governance is not a synonym for multilateralism, although it is a form of multilateralism. In international relations, multilateralism is the 'international governance of the "many"'.[46] According to Keohane, multilateralism is 'the practice of coordinating national policies in groups of three or more states'.[47] Higgott further argued that the reputation gained from multilateralism is generally considered a principal element of global governance.[48] Thus, bilateral and multilateral approaches are differentiated by the institutions and principles governing policy coordination.

China's energy diplomacy

Energy diplomacy has long been an essential tool in China's international energy cooperation efforts because strong political ties are a key foundation for energy cooperation.[49] According to the State Council's 2003 National Energy Strategy and Policy, 'Oil is the key factor in the creation of public wealth' and one of the most crucial commodities in influencing 'global political pattern[s], economic order and military operations.'[50] While energy and political interests have traditionally been intertwined, energy diplomacy refers to the bilateral governmental foreign activities used to secure energy resource supplies and

---

44. Andreas Goldthau, 'The Public Policy Dimension of Energy Security', in *The Routledge Handbook of Energy Security*, ed. Benjamin Sovacool (London: Routledge, 2011), 129–145; Andreas Goldthau and Jan Martin Witte, *Global Energy Governance: The New Rules of the Game* (Washington, DC: Brookings Press, 2010), 99–104; Andreas Goldthau and Jan Martin Witte, 'Back to the Future or Forward to the Past? Strengthening Markets and Rules for Effective Global Energy Governance', *International Affairs* 85, no. 2 (2009): 373–390.
45. Ann Florini and Benjamin Sovacool, 'Bridging the Gaps in Global Energy Governance', *Global Governance* 17, no. 1 (2011): 57–74; Aleh Cherp, Jessica Jewell, and Andreas Goldthau, 'Governing Global Energy: Systems, Transitions, Complexity', *Global Policy* 2, no. 1 (2011): 75–88.
46. Miles Kahler, 'Multilateralism with Small and Large Numbers', *International Organization* 46, no. 3 (1992): 681.
47. Robert Keohane, 'Multilateralism: An Agenda for Research', *Canada's Journal of Global Policy Analysis* 45, no. 4 (1990): 731.
48. Richard Higgott, 'Multilateralism and the Limits of Global Governance', Working Paper No. 134/04, CSGR, 2004.
49. Yishan Xia, senior fellow at the China Institute of International Studies, interview with the author, 2021; Keunwook Paik, senior fellow at Chatham House, interview with the author, 2018. See also Qinhua Xu, 'China's Energy Diplomacy and its Implications for Global Energy Security'. FES Briefing Paper, 2007.
50. PRC State Council, *China's National Energy Strategy and Policy* (Beijing: PRC State Council, 2003).

promote energy business cooperation. It is the bilateral way of energy policy coordination, including diplomatic relations, economic agreement, and FDI, between two countries. It 'differentiates relations case-by-case based principally on a priori particularistic grounds or situational exigencies'.[51]

Energy diplomacy serves as an important tool to achieve national objectives, such as ensuring energy security, managing political risk, expanding international influence, and improving inter-state relations.[52] For example, Most notably, China's ideological concerns for non-political intervention and its ambition to position China as a global player were parts of China's oil diplomacy in Africa.[53] China is widely perceived to be adopting proactive energy diplomacy to purchase energy resources via bilateral ties.[54] China's energy diplomacy was also carried out as a part of its globalisation, as there was a growing need for direct access to overseas energy resources. Chen Huai emphasised that China should attempt to exploit overseas energy resources with its technology and capital instead of merely purchasing them.[55]

Being well aware of the importance of international energy relations, the Chinese government began to develop its energy strategy bilaterally in the 1990s as part of its 'going-out' strategy.[56] China's interaction with both developing and developed countries for accessing resources included strengthening cooperation with countries that produce, transport, and consume oil.[57] This strategy encouraged Chinese companies to invest globally in a broader range of overseas projects and create partnerships with international majors. Chinese NOCs reached out to upstream fields, especially those in the Middle East, Central Asia, Africa, and South America. Besides importing oil and gas in large quantities, these companies became increasingly proactive in overseas mergers and acquisitions. As a result, they emerged as major actors in mergers and acquisitions, with their overseas portfolios expanding. They were also attempting to integrate the midstream and downstream sectors with it in a bundling model to have better control over global supply chains. This was an approach that intended to increase the proportion of Chinese-owned resources in its total imports. Chinese NOCs were particularly interested in partnerships with major international players as a way to share investment risks and gain access to resource-rich regions. Chinese authorities considered it imperative to

---

51. John Ruggie, 'Multilateralism: The Anatomy of an Institution', *International Organization* 46, no. 3 (1992): 561–598.
52. Hamayoun Khan, 'China's Energy Drive and Diplomacy', *International Review* (2008): 91–108.
53. Ian Taylor, 'China's Oil Diplomacy in Africa', *International Affairs* 82, no. 5 (2006): 937–959.
54. David Zweig and Bi Jianhai, 'China's Global Hunt for Energy', *Foreign Affairs* 8, no. 5 (2005): 25–38.
55. EID, 'Chinese Oil Firms "Go out" to Resolve the Oil Predicament', *Economic Information Daily*, 21 September 2004, http://finance.sina.com.cn/g/20040921/08431037218.shtml.
56. Linda Yueh, 'China's "Going Out, Bringing In" Policy: The Geo-economics of China's Rise', *IISS Seminar*, 23–25 March 2012.
57. Ibid.

gain control of overseas resources to guarantee long-term supplies and avoid being overdependent on other actors.

Since China turned into an oil-importing country, diversification of supply, investment, and transit routes have become important tasks for its energy security strategy.[58] The 11th Five-Year Plan stated that the security of China's energy supply should be ensured by expanding international energy cooperation, actively engaging with the international energy system, and making full use of the international market.[59] The actual practice included bilateral cooperation with oil-rich states, the diversification of oil suppliers, the acquisition of overseas oil assets by Chinese national oil companies, the construction of pipelines to tackle the 'Malacca dilemma' (referring to China's need to ship much of its energy resources through the Strait of Malacca), and the modernisation of its navy to protect its sea lanes. Geopolitical tensions over the past decades in the Middle East and the South China Sea have induced China to reduce its reliance on seaborne energy imports and diversify to overland pipeline imports, as reflected by its massive investment in energy pipelines with Russia and Central Asia.[60] The Myanmar-China oil and gas pipeline project was another example of China building an 'emergency lifeline' infrastructure aimed at reducing its reliance on energy imports that transit through strategic chokepoints, such as the Strait of Malacca.

Unlike energy trade, which is negotiated among profit-driven firms through cost-benefit analyses, energy diplomacy is achieved by inter-government agreements and relies on the credibility of states. China's protection of some of its energy trade and investments have also been relying on bilateral means, such as bilateral investment treaties (BITs) and diplomatic ties.[61] Being insistent on state sovereignty, China does not always have full confidence in Western-led institutions protecting its national interests, therefore reshaping its approach towards global energy governance.[62]

China in global energy governance

More recently, in seeking greater protection for its energy supply, China has emphasised the importance of taking a multilateral approach in handling

---

58. PRC State Council, *China's Energy Conditions and Policies* (Beijing: PRC State Council Information Office, 2007); PRC State Council, *China's Energy Policy 2012* (Beijing: PRC State Council Information Office, 2012); PRC State Council, *Energy in China's New Era* (Beijing: PRC State Council Information Office, 2020).
59. PRC State Council, 'The 11th Five-Year Plan for Economic and Social Development of the People's Republic of China (2006–2010)', PRC State Council, 2006, http://www.gov.cn/gongbao/content/2006/content_268766.htm.
60. Chen Weidong and Tom Cutler, 'The Outlook for a Chinese Pivot to Gas', the National Bureau of Asian Research, 2014.
61. China has become one of the largest BIT signers in the world as of 2021.
62. Swaran Singh, 'China's Quest for Multilateralism: Perspectives from India', *Social and Behavioral Science* 2, no. 5 (2010): 720–729.

energy issues.⁶³ Since becoming a net oil importer in 1993, China has become increasingly dependent on the world oil market. As China goes into a deeper process of internationalisation, its foreign trade and investment have also increased substantially and have already touched on the existing international rules and order. Although China has already become one of the largest BIT signers in the world,⁶⁴ it is argued that international law cannot provide China's overseas energy investment with sufficient protection in terms of national treatment standards and arbitration mechanisms. In the BITs signed with major trade partners, such as Australia, Germany, Hong Kong, Russia, Singapore, South Africa, the UK, and the US, national treaties were either non-existent or subject to local law.⁶⁵ Furthermore, some of the international arbitration mechanisms were limited to investor-state dispute settlement. Since there are different laws and regulations in different countries, such inconsistencies reduce the legitimacy of international investment arbitration.⁶⁶ When states realise that bilateral approaches are not sufficient or are too costly to mitigate international issues, they opt for a multilateral approach.

The development of a multilateral approach for energy security was in line with the evolution of Chinese foreign policy, increasingly seeking to regain its centrality over the global governance institutions. China was keen to be part of the global governance system as a way to transform the institutions and norms in favour of Beijing's values and priorities. From the global financial crisis to the COVID-19 pandemic, China had called for global governance to solve the crisis and attempted to show that it had a major role in it. For example, in 2021, Chinese foreign minister Wang Yi emphasised China's effort in promoting the reforms and improvement of the global governance in multiple areas, such as climate, public health, and digital economy.⁶⁷ However, scholars argued that China had been taking a multipronged global governance strategy, selectively supporting institutions that align with its goals and norms.⁶⁸ Among a wide range of global governance issues, energy and climate issues are generally considered to be more 'China-friendly' and require China's contribution. Therefore, compared to other institutions focusing on

---

63. PRC State Council, *China's Energy Conditions and Policies* (Beijing: PRC State Council Information Office, 2007); PRC State Council, *China's Energy Policy 2012* (Beijing: PRC State Council Information Office, 2012); PRC State Council, *Energy in China's New Era* (Beijing: PRC State Council Information Office, 2020).
64. UNCTAD, 'Country-Specific Lists of Bilateral Investment Treaties', United Nations Conference on Trade and Development, 2012, http://unctad.org/en/Pages/DIAE/International%20Investment%20Agreements%20%28IIA%29/Country-specific-Lists-of-BITs.aspx.
65. Former officer from an international energy organisation, interview with the author, 2014.
66. Ibid.
67. PRC MFA, 'China's Diplomacy in 2021: Embracing a Global Vision and Serving the Nation and Its People', PRC MFA, 2021, https://www.fmprc.gov.cn/mfa_eng/wjb_663304/wjbz_663308/2461_663310/202112/t20211220_10471930.html.
68. CFR, 'China's Approach to Global Governance', Council on Foreign Relations, 2021, https://www.cfr.org/china-global-governance/.

controversial issues such as human rights, energy- and climate-related organisations are more well-received by the Chinese government.

Seeking greater protection of its energy supply, China emphasised the importance of a multilateral approach in handling energy issues in the white papers. It first discussed the importance of multilateral cooperation to energy security in the 2007 white paper on 'China's Diplomacy', which explored the high oil prices of the mid-2000s.[69] Subsequently, international energy cooperation via multilateral approaches has been discussed in a number of key policy documents, including China's white papers on energy in 2007,[70] 2012,[71] and 2020[72] as well as in the 2008 white paper on China's diplomacy.[73]

The 2007 white paper,[74] which was China's first white paper on energy, emphasised international energy cooperation via bilateral and multilateral approaches. It also incorporated the ideas of market stability, climate change, and sustainable development into the concept of energy security. This adjustment meant that energy was seen as a vital element that extends beyond the national interests of economic and military power. Although oil supply security still retains a very important position, the government calls for promoting other energy cooperation aspects such as international pricing mechanisms, sustainable environments, solutions for energy-related pollution, and low-carbon economies. In order to achieve the objectives outlined, China emphasises international energy cooperation as an important means. The 2008 white paper on China's diplomacy took a similar stance, reiterating the need for international cooperation in both bilateral approaches and multilateral dialogue to achieve energy security.[75] It noted that China was taking on an increasingly active leadership role in multilateral energy security dialogues.

Alarmed by the global financial crisis of the late 2000s, China decided to intensify its participation in global energy governance initiatives. Senior Chinese leaders have delivered two important public messages on global energy governance. In 2011, the former deputy premier of the State Council, Zeng Peiyan, highlighted that in order to prevent a new global economic crisis caused by sharp fluctuations in the prices of energy and other resources, a stability mechanism in the global energy resource market should be established under the framework of the G20 nations.[76] A year later, during the World

---

69. PRC MFA, *China's Diplomacy* (2007) (Beijing: World Affairs Press, 2007).
70. PRC State Council, *China's Energy Conditions and Policies* (Beijing: PRC State Council Information Office, 2007).
71. PRC State Council, *China's Energy Policy 2012* (Beijing: PRC State Council Information Office, 2012).
72. PRC State Council, *Energy in China's New Era* (Beijing: PRC State Council Information Office, 2020).
73. PRC MFA, *China's Diplomacy (2008)* (Beijing: World Affairs Press, 2008).
74. PRC State Council, *China's Energy Policy 2012* (Beijing: PRC State Council Information Office, 2012).
75. PRC MFA, *China's Diplomacy (2008)* (Beijing: World Affairs Press, 2008).
76. Peiyan Zeng, Speech at BOAO Forum for Asia, Beijing, 26–27 November 2012.

Future Energy Summit in Abu Dhabi, former Premier Wen Jiabao stressed the importance of establishing a global energy market governance mechanism under the framework of the G20 to effectively ensure energy security,[77] which could be achieved by setting up a mechanism that would include energy supplying, consuming, and transiting countries based on a mutual benefit principle. He also highlighted China's wish to 'work with the nations in the world to step up international cooperation and promote sustainable innovation to build a new world with green development and sustainable growth'.

Echoing these two claims, the China Energy White Paper (2012) emphasised global energy governance as a way to address a wide range of energy issues, such as response mechanisms for the global energy market, climate change, sustainable development, technology transfer, and policy coordination.[78] In response to both high oil prices and the global financial crisis, China considered that fair and rational international cooperation was the key to a stable energy market. It stated in a white paper that China's development could not be achieved without cooperation with the rest of the world, and global market stability needs China's input as well.[79] The white paper also called for countries to address energy problems collectively and proposed the establishment of an international institution to govern the energy market. It also promised that China would actively engage in global energy cooperation by focusing on energy resources (e.g., oil, gas, coal, renewable, and nuclear) as well as other local and global externalities, such as climate change and public health.

The government launched the BRI in 2015, which further promoted Chinese energy cooperation in Eurasia as well as China's active role in global energy governance.[80] The energy policy document of the BRI stated that China was developing a new and better energy governance structure. After China signed the Paris Agreement, it pledged to 'build on the Belt and Road energy cooperation system, synchronise countries' effort to jointly build a green and low-carbon global energy governance structure and push forward global green development together'.[81]

China's latest white paper on energy in 2020, and its action plan in 2021 for carbon dioxide peaking before 2030, further expanded the role China could

---

77. UPI, 'China Urges Global Energy Cooperation', *United Press International*, 16 January 2012, http://www.upi.com/Business_News/Energy-Resources/2012/01/16/China-urges-global-energy-cooperation/UPI-77361326740422.
78. PRC State Council, *China's Energy Policy 2012* (Beijing: PRC State Council Information Office, 2012).
79. Ibid.
80. See Chapter 2.
81. PRC NEA, 'Vision and Actions on Energy Cooperation in Jointly Building Silk Road Economic Belt and 21st-Century Maritime Silk Road', PRC NEA, 2017, http://www.nea.gov.cn/2017-05/12/c_136277478.htm.

play in global energy and climate governance.[82] These documents reaffirmed China's willingness to remain an active participant in international energy cooperation in the UN, G20, APEC, and BRICS as well as being a member of international energy organisations, such as IEA, ECT, and IRENA. They also laid out China's attempts to promote low-carbon cooperation under the BRI to improve the connectivity of a green energy infrastructure, carbon pricing system, and green finance. The white paper also called for promoting global energy governance with regional initiations, such as the Shanghai Cooperation Organisation Energy Club,[83] multilateral platforms with Africa,[84] and joint initiation for clean-tech cooperation.[85]

These observations present how China's energy strategy has gradually evolved to incorporate the concept of global energy governance amid the growing concern of climate change. Traditionally, China has preferred bilateral to multilateral approaches in energy cooperation, largely because it can make its own choices within bilateral agreements. China's emphasis on international energy cooperation in the form of multilateralism presents a new outlook for energy security in China and justifies its active role in global energy governance.

---

82. PRC State Council, *Energy in China's New Era* (Beijing: PRC State Council Information Office, 2020), PRC NDRC, 'Action Plan for Carbon Dioxide Peaking before 2030', PRC NDRC, 2021, https://en.ndrc.gov.cn/policies/202110/t20211027_1301020.html.
83. See Chapter 3.
84. See Chapter 4.
85. See Chapter 5.

2
Belt and Road Initiative, AIIB, and Global Energy Governance

In 2015, China launched the Belt and Road Initiative (BRI), its flagship project, which has had serious implications for the country's energy and climate strategy. The initiative was created when China faced increasing pressure of energy import dependency and energy transition.[1] Prioritising infrastructure networks, industrial integration, and sustainable projects, the BRI was expected to enhance China's energy cooperation.[2] Meanwhile, observers have long debated whether the BRI would turn China's energy engagement in the region from its traditional bilateral approach towards a more multilateral approach of global energy governance.[3]

Energy Cooperation in the Belt and Road Initiative

The BRI is a massive development framework with strong geopolitical and economic dimensions, comprising two main components: the land-based Silk Road Economic Belt and the oceanic New Maritime Silk Road. It proposes strengthening the connection among Eurasian countries in five areas: infrastructure, policy, finance, trade, and culture. The BRI represents the revival of the ancient Silk Roads and emphasises 'peace and cooperation, openness

---

1. IEA, 'World Energy Outlook 2021', International Energy Agency, 2021, https://www.iea.org/reports/world-energy-outlook-2021.
2. PRC NEA, 'Vision and Actions on Energy Cooperation in Jointly Building Silk Road Economic Belt and 21st-Century Maritime Silk Road', PRC NDRC, 2017, http://www.nea.gov.cn/2017-05/12/c_136277478.htm.
3. See Philip Andrew-Speed, *Energy Policy and Regulation in the People's Republic of China* (London: Kluwer Law International, 2004), 355–366; Gaye Christoffersen, 'The Role of China in Global Energy Governance', *China Perspectives* 1, no. 2 (2016): 15–24; John Ikenberry, 'The Rise of China and the Future of the West: Can the Liberal System Survive?' *Foreign Affairs* 87, no. 1 (2008): 23–37; Marc Lanteigne, *China and Intl Institutions: Alternative Paths to Global Power* (London: Routledge, 2007), 143–172.

and inclusiveness, mutual learning and mutual benefit'.[4] Geographically, the BRI involves over 60 countries in six economic zones across Eurasia, stretching from Southeast and South Asia to Africa and Europe. Placing China's neighbouring regions, such as Central Asia, as the main strategic priority, the Initiative calls for integration in the region.[5]

Energy cooperation has been repeatedly highlighted in official Chinese BRI documents. In general, energy cooperation in the BRI is aligned with its ambitious economic vision of the opening up of and cooperation among countries located along the Belt and Road.[6] It is a medium for linking Chinese investment 'to a broader Chinese national strategy aimed at forging tighter economic links between China and the rest of Eurasia'.[7] However, the objective of energy cooperation is not merely to acquire energy resources, but also to facilitate the diversification of source and transportation routes, industry development, policy coordination, energy financing, sustainable development, and regional governance in accordance with the Vision and Actions on Energy Cooperation. China's strategic focus has shifted from quantitative objectives (e.g., increasing oil imports and investment) to qualitative objectives (e.g., enhancing its supply chain and sustainability).

Such energy cooperation could support the BRI in addressing a number of interrelated challenges, including China's economic transformation, low-carbon transition, exploration of new markets, managing domestic excess capacity and production, regional security, and growing negativity towards China from its neighbours. Beyond these factors, overseas investments built on energy infrastructures and trade will allow China to bolster and solidify its geopolitical standing. Its focus on green development and environment-friendly projects will also make the Initiative a multilateral cooperation platform for tackling climate change.[8] The Chinese government emphasised that strengthening energy cooperation by jointly building the BRI can 'stimulate wider and deeper regional cooperation at a higher level for the economic

---

4. PRC NDRC, PRC MFA, and PRC MOFCOM, 'Vision and Actions on Jointly Building the Silk Road Economic Belt and the 21st-Century Maritime Silk Road', PRC NDRC, 2015, https://www.fmprc.gov.cn/eng/topics_665678/2015zt/xjpcxbayzlt2015nnh/201503/t20150328_705553.html.
5. Pepe Escobar, 'The Eurasian Big Bang: How China and Russia Are Carving Out Their Own World Order', *Energy Post*, 25 August 2015; Wenjie Chen, David Dollar, and Heiwai Tang, 'Why Is China Investing in Africa? Evidence from the Firm Level', *World Bank Economic Review* 32, no. 3 (2018): 610–632.
6. PRC NEA, 'Vision and Actions on Energy Cooperation in Jointly Building Silk Road Economic Belt and 21st-Century Maritime Silk Road', PRC NDRC, 2017, http://www.nea.gov.cn/2017-05/12/c_136277478.htm.
7. Erica Downs, 'Mission Mostly Accomplished: China's Energy Trade and Investment along the Silk Road Economic Belt', *China Brief* 15, no. 6 (2015): 3–6.
8. PRC NDRC, 'Action Plan for Carbon Dioxide Peaking before 2030', PRC NDRC, 2021, https://en.ndrc.gov.cn/policies/202110/t20211027_1301020.html.

prosperity of the whole world'.[9] In terms of connectivity, energy cooperation in the BRI is expected to be an integrated and multilateral engagement strategy.

Five aspects of energy cooperation

Energy cooperation, which is multidimensional in nature, covers at least five areas of connectivity in the BRI. The implementation of energy cooperation is widely considered to be rooted in the following aspects.

Energy infrastructure

China has been expanding the scale of investment in energy projects to facilitate further connectivity of infrastructures in the BRI.[10] Energy cooperation is not merely concerned with the trading of energy resources or asset acquisition, but it also often includes investment in infrastructures, such as refineries, power plants, solar panels, oil and gas pipelines, and power transmission corridors. Other than energy facilities, energy projects usually include other logistical infrastructures, such as roads, railways, port hubs, and storage facilities. Thus, energy projects—especially those involving massive infrastructures—are a promising means for the BRI. The BRI has identified the enormous demand for energy infrastructure among the regions it covers. These areas, including Russia, Central Asia, and the Middle East, are rich in resources such as oil and gas. Energy trade, industrialisation, urbanisation, and development in these regions all require infrastructures in various sectors, ranging from fossil fuel energy to renewable energies. Considering the transnational scale of these energy projects, energy cooperation within the BRI is expected to develop an infrastructure network for economic advancement in Eurasia.

Industrial integration

One of the BRI's key areas of focus is creating an integrated industrial value chain of energy. This connectivity will rely on the deep integration of markets, efficient allocation of resources, and cooperation in technology, equipment, and engineering services in the energy sector. China is attempting to 'increase cooperation in the exploration and development of coal, oil, gas, metal minerals and other conventional energy sources' and 'promote cooperation in the processing and conversion of energy and resources at or near places where

---

9. PRC NDRC, PRC MFA, and PRC MOFCOM, 'Vision and Actions on Jointly Building the Silk Road Economic Belt and the 21st-Century Maritime Silk Road', PRC NDRC, 2015, https://www.fmprc.gov.cn/eng/topics_665678/2015zt/xjpcxbayzlt2015nnh/201503/t20150328_705553.html.
10. G. Feng, *Annual Report on China's Outbound Direct Investment and Host Country Risks* (Beijing: Social Sciences Academic Press, 2017).

they are exploited'.[11] With a massive amount of capital, Chinese companies are in a good position to merge with organisations and acquire the energy assets found along the BRI. China can also drive the development of energy-related industries, such as fertilisers, agriculture, irrigation, and domestic gas sales, which would be an effective way to expand and integrate energy facilities and markets in the upstream, midstream, and downstream sectors. Other than promoting the domestic economic development of recipient countries, such an approach can also help establish hubs in important regions and further enhance security in the regions along the BRI.

Trade and investment

Connectivity in trade and investment is a major goal in energy cooperation under the BRI. In 2016, oil imported from regions along the BRI accounted for approximately 65% of the country's supply.[12] China will continue to expand trade in energy through investment. Energy, transportation, and telecommunications are the key sectors of Chinese FDI in the BRI. Chinese energy investment primarily targets regions in Southeast, Central, and South Asia, all of which are near China.[13] Countries in these regions are complementary to China in terms of economic development stages and energy resources, thus enhancing the connectivity among their industries. To deepen energy investment cooperation, China encourages companies to adopt various measures, including direct investment, mergers and acquisitions, and public-private partnerships (PPPs).

Financial institutions

Due to their scale, energy projects always come with massive investments. The Chinese government 'will enhance the involvement of financial institutions in the lifecycle of energy cooperation projects to create [a] sound energy "industry plus finance" cooperation pattern'.[14] Chinese financial institutions, such as the China Development Bank (CDB), the Agricultural Development Bank, and the Export-Import Bank of China, as well as newly established institutes in the BRI, such as the Asia Infrastructure Investment Bank (AIIB) and

---

11. PRC NEA, 'Vision and Actions on Energy Cooperation in Jointly Building Silk Road Economic Belt and 21st-Century Maritime Silk Road', PRC NDRC, 2017, http://www.nea.gov.cn/2017-05/12/c_136277478.htm.
12. G. Feng, *Annual Report on China's Outbound Direct Investment and Host Country Risks* (Beijing: Social Sciences Academic Press, 2017).
13. For example, the China–Central Asia gas pipeline, the China-Russia gas pipeline, and various solar and water power projects in the China-Pakistan Economic Corridor.
14. PRC NEA, 'Vision and Actions on Energy Cooperation in Jointly Building Silk Road Economic Belt and 21st-Century Maritime Silk Road', PRC NDRC, 2017, http://www.nea.gov.cn/2017-05/12/c_136277478.htm.

the Silk Road Fund (SRF), play crucial roles in the energy investment in the BRI. The BRI has brought the above financial institutions and their combined commercial strategy and development policies to the region. Chinese financial institutions, particularly the CDB, have financed a wide range of Chinese energy investments overseas in the past and have entered partnerships with foreign governments and companies from over 140 countries.[15] Chinese financial institutions provide energy-backed loans to foreign governments and energy companies in resource-rich regions. The loans normally include agreements about the revenue from the oil business and require borrowers to use Chinese equipment.

Sustainable development

The Chinese government claims that the BRI will be a green and efficient initiative. Ever since China signed the Paris Agreement in 2016, Chinese authorities have sought to accommodate climate finance and sustainable development under the framework of the BRI. According to the Vision and Actions on Energy Cooperation, energy cooperation under the BRI 'must attach great importance to the issue of environmental protection in the process of energy development, and strive to encourage the efficient development and utilisation of clean energy'.[16] China claims that it 'will strictly control the emission of pollutants and greenhouse gases, raise energy efficiency and contribute to green and efficient development in all countries [that participate in the BRI]'.[17] Its Action Plan for Carbon Dioxide Peaking Before 2030 also stressed that China will 'strengthen cooperation with other participants on green infrastructure, green energy, and green finance' and will 'make overseas projects more environmentally sustainable'.[18] These statements implied that certain environmental conditions would be included in the BRI-led energy investments. An expansion of the investment in renewable energy projects, such as solar power and power transmission lines, can enhance connectivity in the region. Institutionally, China seeks to promote clean energy and infrastructural investment via the AIIB as well as other platforms such as the BRI International Green Development Coalition.

---

15. Alessandro Provaggi, 'China Development Bank's Financing Mechanisms: Focus on Foreign Investments', Global Projects Center (Working Paper, Stanford University, 2013); Daniel Rosen and Thilo Hanemann, *China invests in Europe: Patterns, Impacts and Policy Implications* (New York: Rhodium Group, 2012).
16. PRC NEA, 'Vision and Actions on Energy Cooperation in Jointly Building Silk Road Economic Belt and 21st-Century Maritime Silk Road', PRC NDRC, 2017, http://www.nea.gov.cn/2017-05/12/c_136277478.htm.
17. Ibid.
18. PRC NDRC, 'Action Plan for Carbon Dioxide Peaking before 2030', PRC NDRC, 2021, https://en.ndrc.gov.cn/policies/202110/t20211027_1301020.html.

These five points showed that energy cooperation plays an important role in strengthening connectivity under the BRI because it involves an ambitious programme of infrastructure construction, resource trade, energy finance products, green development, and energy governance.[19] Official Chinese documents on the BRI have repeatedly highlighted the importance of energy cooperation. Most notably, the 2015 'Vision and Actions on Jointly Building the Silk Road Economic Belt and the 21st-Century Maritime Silk Road' identified energy cooperation as an important aspect in achieving the goals of the BRI. The 2016 '13th Five-Year Plan for Economic and Social Development' addressed the role of international energy cooperation in the BRI's economic corridors and promised that China would 'strengthen international cooperation on energy and resources and production chains, and increase local processing and conversion'.[20] The '13th Five-Year Plan for Energy Development' further confirmed the importance of energy cooperation within the BRI and stated that, through BRI-related energy projects, China would enhance the connectivity of the energy infrastructure in Eurasia and participate to a greater extent in global energy governance.

In 2017, the 'Vision and Actions on Energy Cooperation in Jointly Building the Silk Road Economic Belt and the 21st-Century Maritime Silk Road' outlined the scope and principles of energy cooperation, emphasising the integration of regional markets and the promotion of a universal, rules-based, open, non-discriminatory, and equitable multilateral trading system. The Chinese government stated that China was seeking 'a more open and efficient international cooperation platform; a closer, stronger partnership network; and to push for a more just, reasonable, and balanced international governance system'.[21] More recently, China's Action plan for carbon dioxide peaking before 2030 and latest energy white paper in 2020—Energy in China's New Era—emphasised the role of enhancing global governance in China's energy security and green development.[22] With the BRI, the aims of China's energy deals have shifted from quantitative objectives, such as the volume of energy imported, to qualitative objectives, such as upgrading value chains and infrastructure networks.[23] It also paved the way for greater involvement in global energy governance, particularly via the establishment of the AIIB.

---

19. Kaho Yu, 'Energy Cooperation in the Belt and Road Initiative: EU Experience of the Trans-European Networks for Energy', *Asia Europe Journal* 16, no. 3 (2018): 251–265.
20. PRC State Council, 'The 13th Five-Year Plan for Economic and Social Development of the People's Republic of China (2016–2020)', PRC State Council, 2016, https://en.ndrc.gov.cn/policies/202105/P020210527785800103339.pdf.
21. Shaohui Tian, 'China Focus: What to Expect from Belt and Road Forum', *Xinhua News*, 1 May 2017.
22. PRC State Council, *Energy in China's New Era* (Beijing: PRC State Council Information Office, 2020); PRC NDRC, 'Action Plan for Carbon Dioxide Peaking before 2030', PRC NDRC, 2021, https://en.ndrc.gov.cn/policies/202110/t20211027_1301020.html.
23. Kaho Yu, 'The Geopolitics of Energy Cooperation in China's Belt and Road Initiative', *NBR Special Report* 68 (2017): 29–39.

AIIB and Global Energy Governance

The establishment of the AIIB is considered as the institutionalisation of China's BRI cooperation as well as its role in global energy governance. The AIIB is a multilateral development bank (MDB) that focuses on infrastructure development, economic integration, green development, and interconnectivity in Asia. Its establishment was announced by President Xi Jinping during his visit to Southeast Asia in 2013. The AIIB began operations with US$100 billion in capital after the agreement was ratified in 2015.[24] By 2017, the AIIB had grown to 61 members and 23 prospective members, including a number of non-Asian countries such as the UK, Germany, and Brazil.[25] A wide base of member countries from Asia, Europe, the Middle East, and Africa is the major source of legitimacy for the AIIB; this wide-scale membership has helped to build China's confidence.[26] As a multilateral bank with multiple stakeholders, the AIIB automatically reinforces multilateralism since it is not easy for China alone to exert influence over the decisions of the bank.[27]

In response to the Paris Agreement as well as the energy needs of developing countries, the AIIB developed its own energy strategy to facilitate a sustainable energy investment largely funded by China.[28] Following the AIIB's core values of 'lean, clean, and green', the AIIB's energy strategy is a framework for the bank to support its member countries to 'develop and improve their energy infrastructure, increase energy access, and facilitate their transition to a less carbon-intensive energy mix'.[29] The energy strategy has three priorities: sustainable infrastructure, cross-country connectivity, and private capital mobilisation.

South-South cooperation is a key element in the BRI, and the AIIB is in a strong position to carve out a new niche of multilateral cooperation in sustainable development in the global South. While the AIIB is committed to upholding the Paris Agreement's climate goals and the Sustainable Development Goals (SDGs), its investments as of 2018 (listed in Table 1) have embraced sustainable energy. The AIIB has followed the intention of its energy strategy

---

24. AIIB, 'AIIB Annual Report and Accounts 2016', Asian Infrastructure Investment Bank, 2016, https://www.aiib.org/en/news-events/annual-report/2016/home/pdf/Annual_Report_2016.pdf.
25. AIIB, 'AIIB Annual Report and Accounts 2017', Asian Infrastructure Investment Bank, 2017, https://www.aiib.org/en/news-events/annual-report/2017/_common/pdf/AIIB-Annual-Report-2017.pdf.
26. Gui Qing Koh, 'How China Decided to Redraw the Global Financial Map', *Reuters*, 17 September 2015.
27. G.-F. Legault, 'AIIB Melding, Not Moulding Global Governance', East Asia Forum, 2015, http://www.eastasiaforum.org/2015/11/18/aiib-melding-not-moulding-global-governance.
28. AIIB, 'Energy Sector Strategy: Sustainable Energy for Asia', Asian Infrastructure Investment Bank, 2017, https://www.aiib.org/en/policies-strategies/strategies/sustainable-energy-asia/index.html.
29. AIIB, 'Energy Sector Strategy: Sustainable Energy for Asia', 10.

by limiting lending for fossil fuels in favour of sustainable energy options.[30] Many countries along the BRI have low-lying topography and face significant threats from climate change. China's transformation into the world's largest energy consumer and greenhouse gas emitter has already placed it in top energy and climate agendas, such as meeting global energy demands, reducing greenhouse gas emissions, and transitioning to a low-carbon economy. Ever since China signed the Paris Agreement, the nation has strived to accommodate climate finance and sustainable development under the BRI framework. According to the 'Vision and Actions', BRI-related energy cooperation must 'attach great importance to the issue of environmental protection in the process of energy development, and strive to encourage the efficient development and utilisation of clean energy'.[31]

Institutionally, the AIIB provides a platform for China to promote a clean, sustainable infrastructure by attaching conditions related to the environment to its investments.[32] By looking into the AIIB's energy-investment portfolio, Oxfam pointed out that the bank provided a major opportunity to chart a new path of sustainable development in the global South, which differs from existing MDBs in at least four ways.[33] First, the AIIB is the first major MDB in which developing countries hold a majority of shares; hence, compared with existing MDBs such as the World Bank and the ADB, the AIIB's decision making is generally expected to align more closely with the needs of developing countries. Second, for various bureaucracy-related reasons, existing MDBs have been slow to transfer loans for energy projects on the scale required. Third, while the fossil fuel projects of existing MDBs are ongoing, AIIB emphasise investment with conditions attached to low-carbon and environmental protection. Fourth, it takes time for existing MDBs to reform their structures and financing tools.

Regions under the BRI are unevenly developed, often with regressive energy infrastructures. According to the World Bank Enterprise Survey, several Eurasian countries, including Afghanistan, Bangladesh, Georgia, Iraq, and Pakistan, are currently undergoing urbanisation and industrialisation and continue to suffer from unreliable electricity services.[34] These areas

---

30. Especially hydropower and gas. Gas is cleaner than coal and is generally considered to be transit options to renewable energy.
31. PRC NEA, 'Vision and Actions on Energy Cooperation in Jointly Building Silk Road Economic Belt and 21st-Century Maritime Silk Road', PRC NDRC, 2017, http://www.nea.gov.cn/2017-05/12/c_136277478.htm.
32. AIIB, 'Energy Sector Strategy: Sustainable Energy for Asia', Asian Infrastructure Investment Bank, 2017, https://www.aiib.org/en/policies-strategies/strategies/sustainable-energy-asia/index.html.
33. Oxfam, 'The AIIB's Energy Opportunity: How the Asian Infrastructure Investment Bank's Energy Lending Can Chart a New Path of Sustainable Development', Oxfam, 2017, https://www.oxfam.org/sites/www.oxfam.org/files/file_attachments/bn-the-aiibs-energy-opportunity-150617-en.pdf.
34. World Bank, 'World Bank Enterprise Survey', World Bank, 2021, https://www.enterprisesurveys.org/en/enterprisesurveys.

require investments in building new and upgrading old infrastructures. A lack of access (or unreliable access) to energy services forces households to rely on traditional biomass combustion, which exposes the populations here to indoor pollution and other devastating health effects. Additionally, the use of renewable energy is relatively low in the regions of the BRI, which implies a demand for infrastructure for renewable power. The long-term climate goals provided in the Paris Agreement match China's growing desire for overseas renewables investment. Highlighting both infrastructural demands and sustainable development in Asia, the AIIB is committed to promoting access to modern energy, the reliability of electricity supply, and the reduction of the energy supply's carbon intensity.

Although MDBs have supported energy investment, private capital investments for energy projects in developing Asian countries remain marginal. In order to bridge the infrastructure investment gaps within developing Asian nations and deepen energy investment cooperation, the AIIB is committed to adopting various measures, including direct investment, mergers and acquisitions, and PPPs. In the energy sector, the PPP model is feasible in transferring risks to social capital with a division of labour in which the government offers political support for the project, while the private sector takes care of project construction and operation.

The bank has been investing in cross-border energy projects and trade of electricity and energy resources.[35] In other words, the energy investment of the AIIB relies on regional integration and cooperation. This is a way to increase the market size, improve competitiveness, and connect regions. While the development of the electricity network contributes to more efficient electricity generation and the use of renewable energy, the development of gas networks can increase the flexibility and security of energy access. The promotion of interconnectivity of Asian energy systems, especially power and gas, can help the region address the policy challenges of market competitiveness, climate change, and supply security. More importantly, it will also likely strengthen the global role of China.

The investment scale of the BRI further expands this need for investment protection. The Chinese government has stated that China was looking for 'a more open and efficient international cooperation platform; a closer, stronger partnership network; and to push for a more just, reasonable, and balanced international governance system'.[36] The establishment of the AIIB reflects China's hesitation to rely solely on existing international organisations led by the West in the region, such as the World Bank, the Asian Development Bank, and the Energy Charter. Therefore, China has instead learned from the experience of these organisations and has advocated that the AIIB could

---

35. See Appendix, Table 1, for energy projects funded by the AIIB from 2015 to 2017.
36. Shaohui Tian, 'China Focus: What to Expect from Belt and Road Forum', *Xinhua News*, 1 May 2017, http://news.xinhuanet.com/english/2017-05/01/c_136248648.htm.

develop both competitive and cooperative relationships with existing institutes, thereby reshaping the political and economic dynamics among several Eurasian regions.

China's View towards International Energy Organisations

Following its emergence as the world's largest energy consumer and contributor of greenhouse gases, China has pledged its support to the international energy and climate agenda, particularly concerning global energy security, climate change mitigation, and transitioning to a low-carbon economy. While China is influenced by other countries in global energy governance, its behaviour towards multilateralism also directs the development of global energy governance. The question then remains about the extent to which China would align with existing global energy governance.

In general, China has proactively participated in and joined a number of international energy organisations. Both the BRI and latest official documents have emphasised China's involvement in global energy governance, especially its partnership with international energy organisations. The action plan for carbon dioxide peaking before 2030 also highlighted climate platforms initiated by China, such as the Belt and Road South-South Cooperation Initiative on Climate Change and the Belt and Road Science, Technology, and Innovation Cooperation Action Plan. These approaches are in line with the development of Chinese foreign policy that aims to secure a larger role for itself in multiple international institutions. China has developed different levels of engagement with major international organisations, either as a founder, member, partner country, observer, or associate. These organisations include the World Energy Council, the IEA, the International Energy Forum, the Organization of the Petroleum Exporting Countries, the Energy Charter, the International Atomic Energy Agency, and the International Renewable Energy Agency. China has also contributed to the global energy debate in the context of international and regional organisations, such as the G20 countries, BRICS, Asia-Pacific Economic Cooperation, and Shanghai Cooperation Organisation.

However, these affiliations do not naturally equate to a full acceptance of the existing global energy governance structure. While China has attempted to fulfil its commitments to these institutions, it has been reluctantly taking on imposed responsibilities that are not in line with its values and priorities; for example, the need to speed up fading coal consumption. In a Brooking's report, Gross pointed out how China has become a key player in the global energy transition, but at the same time, has to rely on fossil fuels for energy security.

> As energy demand growth has slowed elsewhere, over the last decade China's energy demand has increased by nearly 50%. Gross explores the electricity and oil and gas industries separately to understand how China

carves out a place in energy markets and how it might change its policies as it confronts the challenges of climate change and local pollution. China aims to lead in new energy technologies in electricity, and has succeeded in leading the world in its pace of solar and wind capacity buildout. However, China is still reliant on oil and gas imports as domestic production cannot keep up with its voracious demand. As demand for coal-fired plants slows in China, Beijing has financed coal-fired power projects abroad through the BRI to keep excess Chinese industrial capacity working.[37]

Similarly, China has mixed views regarding its involvement in international energy organisations, especially the rival-led ones. When China initially engaged in global energy governance in the 1980s by joining the World Energy Council, the Chinese government was not completely familiar with international rules and had concerns about the political risks involved in joining such organisations in general. China's leadership was concerned that its national interests would be compromised.[38] Joining these international energy organisations would imply that China was bound by an energy governance system dominated by its potential rivals. As a result, China has remained hesitant to fully accept the existing international standards and legal requirements, and it has taken cautious steps to explore the international system. Chinese stakeholders understand that the intention of the international system and treaties is to protect investment, but they have also pointed out that these could be restrictive for China. There are worries about whether China can always meet the requirements pre-set in the existing treaties, and that failure to do so could result in disputes or penalties. They are also concerned that the host countries could use these standards as a bargaining tool against China. Their hesitation reflects China's scepticism towards international systems dominated by rivals and insistence on state sovereignty.

A study by the Grantham Institute and the Energy Research Institute of China's NRDC indicated the prevailing idea that in the past, China generally had little say in global energy issues due to limited experience with global energy governance.[39] China did not have a strong voice in international energy issues, such as in price setting and emergency responses.[40] China seldom got its way in negotiations in international energy cooperation and was rarely able to appeal successfully on legal grounds during disputes.[41] Besides, Chinese stakeholders had little experience of how to utilise international organisations

---

37. Samantha Gross, 'Global China: Global Governance and Norms', Brookings Institute, 2021, https://www.brookings.edu/research/global-china-global-governance-and-norms/.
38. IEA, 'China's Engagement in Global Energy Governance', OECD, 2015, https://www.oecd.org/publications/china-s-engagement-in-global-energy-governance-9789264255845-en.htm.
39. Energy Research Institute and Grantham Institute, *Global Energy Governance Reform and China's Participation: Consultation Draft Report* (London: Grantham Institute, 2014).
40. Ibid.
41. Former officer from an international energy organisation, interview with the author, 2014.

or treaties, such as the World Oil Council, IEA, or Energy Charter Treaty, to resolve disputes.[42]

For instance, in November 2017, CNPC issued a warning that there was a drastic decline in the natural gas supply from Turkmenistan and that domestic gas sales would be cut by about 10 million cubic meters in the northern regions of China.[43] The fall in gas imports exacerbated the imbalance between supply and demand in the Chinese gas market and sparked widespread public complaints.[44] Eventually, the dispute was resolved through diplomatic and political measures. The incident demonstrated that China was not prepared to prevent or resolve energy cooperation disputes via multilateral institutions. Indeed, all energy policy white papers in 2007, 2012, and 2020 indicate that the bilateral approach remains key in Chinese energy strategy, especially during supply chain disruption or a geopolitical crisis.

The multilateral approach is more likely to be a strategic tool in the broader Chinese energy diplomacy, supporting its bilateral energy relations. China has traditionally considered bilateral strategies to be more efficient and flexible and has preferred bilateral to multilateral approaches in its energy cooperation endeavours.[45] With fewer parties involved, coordination costs are lower, and China can maximise national benefits through bilateral cooperation. Additionally, different regions have varying histories, cultures, domestic politics, and economic development levels, which bilateral approaches can often address more directly.[46] On some occasions, the multilateral approach has even become a cover for China's bilateral energy diplomacy. Blanchard indicated that 'national interests seem to explain much of China's devotion to multilateralism or, where relevant, the lack thereof'.[47]

Despite its pledge to participate in global energy governance, China appears to be cautious in its participation in international energy organisations led by rivals and avoids blindly aligning with their underlying ideology.[48]

---

42. Ibid.
43. Global Times, 'China Searches for Solution after Being Hit by Natural Gas Shortage', *Global Times*, 1 January 2018, http://www.globaltimes.cn/content/1083117.shtml.
44. Ibid.
45. Daojiong Zha and Suetyi Lai, 'EU-China Energy Governance: What Lessons to Be Drawn?', in *Challenges of European External Energy Governance with Emerging Powers*, ed. Michele Knodt and Nadine Piefer (Surrey: Ashgate, 2015), 129–138.
46. Janice K. M. Heppell, 'Confidence-Building Measures: Bilateral versus Multilateral Approaches', in *Peace and Security in Northeast Asia: The Nuclear Issue and the Korean Peninsula*, ed. Yong Whan Kihl and Peter Hayers (London: Routledge, 1997), 270.
47. Jean-Marc Blanchard, 'Harmonious World and China's Foreign Economic Policy: Features, Implications, and Challenges', *Journal of Chinese Political Science* 13, no. 2 (2008): 165–192, 174.
48. For example, China remains an observer of the Energy Charter partly because a full membership requires the ratification of the Energy Charter Treaty (ECT), which could involve potential political risks. In other words, China wants to remain unobligated and to be able to 'exit' whenever it feels it is necessary to do so. Chinese authorities were alarmed by the 2014 Yukos lawsuit filed under the ECT against the Russian government. The authorities thus paid attention to the risk of signing the ECT rather than how the ECT could protect

While technical barriers to joining some international energy organisations exist, for example, the requirement of being a member of the Organisation for Economic Co-operation and Development (OECD) to join IEA, there are also political risk concerns for China to join and play a 'game' dominated by Western countries. Geopolitical tensions, negative perception towards China, and Western restrictions imposed on Chinese investment have further complicated China's involvement in existing global energy governance.

A common viewpoint shared by Chinese authorities is that China should follow its own development path rather than a Western one. Such a statement implies that there could be an 'ideological gap' between the West and China in how they understand global energy governance and China's role in it. For example, while it is generally understood that global energy governance is 'the setting and enforcement of rules and regulations for global collective energy interests',[49] it could be difficult for China to fully align with some controversial ones set by rivals due to ideological differences. However, this does not mean that China is closing its door to global energy governance. Instead, Chinese authorities are seeking an entry point to project China's influence on global energy governance to make the environment more favourable for the country, especially in emerging markets and climate-related areas. The BRI has demonstrated how China has created a niche for itself in global energy governance.

Belt and Road Investment and Global Energy Governance

Instead of isolating itself from international energy organisations, China has been proactively participating in global energy governance, especially in areas where multilateral energy relations have emerged, such as climate, energy markets, gas and oil pipeline systems, cross-border electricity transmission grids, and technology transfers. These needs have been further expanded by the investment scale and climate commitment of the BRI.

Considering the scale of BRI-related energy cooperation in terms of geography and investment, the risk assessment and protection of energy investment under this Initiative require effective multilateral mechanisms. The Chinese government faces a complicated situation involving the potential need for a multilateral approach for increasing energy investments as well as its general hesitation towards existing international institutions. Although the BRI presents clear opportunities for Chinese companies, the road ahead will likely be bumpy. Investment and development in the Eurasian region involve

---

the investment or the company. The authorities also expressed concern about whether the Chinese government might be exposed to similar potential lawsuits that the Russian government had faced.

49. Bo Kong, 'Governing China's Energy in the Context of Global Governance', *Global Policy* 2, no. 1 (2011): 51–65.

a certain degree of risk, and it will be necessary to create a web of investment-treaty protections to reduce the risks involved.

Similarly, climate commitment of China requires strong financing that relies on multilateral collaboration in structuring lending packets to meet the need of borrowing countries in dealing with high cost of energy transition. Increasing climate risks have also driven Chinese creditors, such as China Development Bank, to adopt global standards, such as the UN Global Company principles, in their environmental assessment system for investment. Moreover, China has also been promoting climate cooperation via China-initiated platforms; for example, the BRI International Green Development Coalition, the Belt and Road South-South Cooperation Initiative on Climate Change, and the Belt and Road Science, Technology, and Innovation Cooperation Action Plan.

A number of multilateral mechanisms have already been developed to mitigate risk, but they are insufficient to protect Chinese investments in the region. A study by the Energy Charter Secretariat argues that 'as more and more Chinese energy investments flow into Eurasian countries, there is a potential risk that those investments might be blocked by unfair and/or discriminatory treatments imposed by the host countries. A certain amount of Chinese multilateral cooperative frameworks or mechanisms that exist in the Central Asian region are not legally binding. Thus far, political conciliation and diplomatic mediation are the most frequently used measures in the case of energy investment disputes or transit interruptions.'[50]

China had joined international energy organisations at different levels or set up mechanisms of cooperation with these organisations. The Chinese NOCs on the front line would likely show more interest in international energy treaties, such as the Energy Charter Treaty, because they are aware of the multinational pipeline risks in Central Asia, which such a treaty could potentially reduce.[51] As far as disagreements over oil and gas transits are concerned (e.g., the gas shortage in the winter of 2017 due to a sharp fall in the volume of pipeline gas supplied from Central Asia), the existing legal mechanisms appear to be inadequate to ensure the timely settlement of disputes. Although China traditionally prefers to engage in bilateralism, it may have to turn to a multilateral approach once the realisation sets in that the risk management of its cross-border energy infrastructure (e.g., the Central Asia pipeline project) depends on multilateralism.[52]

China's engagement with towards the Energy Charter Treaty has indicated its attitude towards global energy governance. Currently, while China holds an observer status of the Energy Charter Treaty, most of the countries involved in the BRI—mostly from Europe and Central Asia—have ratified the Treaty. It

---

50. Zhuwei Wang, 'Securing Energy Flows from Central Asia to China: Relevance of the Energy Charter Treaty', (Brussel: Energy Charter Secretariat, 2014).
51. Kaho Yu, 'Energy Cooperation under the Belt and Road Initiative: Implications for Global Energy Governance', *The Journal of World Investment & Trade* 20, no. 2–3 (2019): 243–258.
52. Ibid.

means that full membership in the Energy Charter Treaty could further protect Chinese trade, investment, and the transportation of energy resources in the BRI. However, although cooperation between the Energy Charter and China has so far been fairly stable and mutually beneficial, the Chinese authorities are still hesitant to join the European-led institution. Zhang Libin, a Beijing-based lawyer, has pointed out that the Chinese authorities may doubt whether international institutions like the Energy Charter can protect their national interests.[53] They tend to focus on the risks of signing the Energy Charter Treaty instead of considering how it can protect investments and companies. In particular, the Chinese authorities were alarmed by the news that the Energy Charter Treaty had been used in the Yukos case in 2014.[54] They feared that the Chinese government might face similar punishment to that threatened against the Russian government in that case. In contrast, the Chinese authorities were comfortable signing the International Energy Charter in 2015, which is a political declaration for strengthening energy cooperation among the signatory member states and does not bear any legally binding obligation.[55] In other words, despite its efforts in promoting global energy governance, China wishes to remain unfettered by obligations and to be able to 'exit' whenever it feels compelled to do so.

Therefore, while governing energy issues via the BRI will likely follow the path of existing international organisations, such as the IEA or the Energy Charter Treaty,[56] China appears to be more interested in the establishment of a more China-led institute to manage its energy problems.[57] Indeed, Beijing has opted to establish its own Chinese- or Asian-led regional institutions, such as the AIIB, the Silk Road Fund, BRI Energy Partnership network, or the Shanghai Cooperation Organisation.[58] These organisations and platforms may either cooperate or compete with existing institutions. Although such a process may take years, it will eventually impact the role of the existing institutions and rebalance global energy governance.

---

53. Asia Law, 'Risks for Chinese Investors in the One Belt One Road Initiative', *Asialaw*, 2016, https://www.asialaw.com/articles/risks-for-chinese-investors-in-the-one-belt-one-road-initiative/armhdfdc.
54. Kaho Yu, 'Energy Cooperation under the Belt and Road Initiative: Implications for Global Energy Governance', *The Journal of World Investment & Trade* 20, no. 2–3 (2019): 243–258.
55. See Energy Charter, 'The International Energy Charter', Energy Charter, 2015, https://www.energycharter.org/process/international-energy-charter-2015/overview/.
56. Gaye Christoffersen, 'The Role of China in Global Energy Governance', *China Perspectives* 1, no. 2 (2016): 15–24.
57. Kaho Yu, 'Energy Cooperation under the Belt and Road Initiative: Implications for Global Energy Governance', *The Journal of World Investment & Trade* 20, no. 2–3 (2019): 243–258.
58. In the past, China tried to diversify its energy suppliers and secure access to oil and gas fields via the Shanghai Cooperation Organisation Energy Club, which was initiated in 2006. See Elzbieta Maria Pron, 'China's Energy Diplomacy via the Shanghai Cooperation Organisation', in *Energy Security and Sustainable Economic Growth in China*, ed. Shujie Yao and Maria Jesus Herrerias (London: Palgrave Macmillan, 2014), 52–73.

3
China–Central Asia Energy Cooperation

A Transnational Infrastructure Network of Oil and Gas Pipelines

The China-Central Asia energy cooperation dates back to the early 1990s and is the backbone of energy diplomacy in China's 'going-out' strategy and BRI. Since the abundant production of oil and gas in Central Asia is in stark contrast with their limited oil and gas consumption ability, the region has a large amount of surplus oil and gas available for export. A complementary supply-demand relationship between China and Central Asia has maintained their bilateral oil and gas trade over the last two decades. While China has attempted to secure supply to meet its growing domestic energy demand, it is also trying to strengthen regional relations for national security and geopolitical reasons. A stable and peaceful external environment, especially border issues and regional security, is necessary for its rapid economic development.[1]

China's interests in its relations with Central Asia are intimately connected to its diplomacy in these regions. Since the fall of the Soviet Union, China has shown its intent to develop greater economic and trade relations with the newly independent states, particularly Kazakhstan, through border trade and infrastructural links.[2] The key commodities in this Silk Road are no longer silk, as it was in the past, but oil and gas. This approach has ultimately enmeshed China in the wider geopolitical competition for its access to Central Asia's oil and gas and greater political and economic influence in the region. China's reorientation of its energy strategy towards Central Asia in the early 1990s was more of a strategic manoeuvre than a 'market' approach to oil and gas resources.[3] For the same reason, Central Asia remains a priority region in China's BRI. However, this does not necessarily mean that energy security is merely a part of China's political manoeuvre in the region. The energy supply from Central

---

1. Ross H. Munro, 'China's Relations with Its Neighbours', *International Journal* 61, no. 2 (2006): 320–328, 327.
2. Ibid.
3. Ibid.

Asia was also used to mitigate China's growing demand pressure driven by rapid economic development, high oil prices, and its increasing dependency on Middle Eastern energy sources.

Two key elements in their energy cooperation are the transnational pipeline projects and the Shanghai Cooperation Organization (SCO). They do not merely indicate the development and changes in the energy cooperation mechanism between China and Central Asia; they also reveal the rationale underpinning the region's Chinese energy security. The necessity to diversify its energy suppliers is also a determining factor for the reorientation of China's foreign energy policy towards Central Asia. Since energy interdependence continues to strengthen, diplomacy has become an important means to promote energy cooperation. To ensure a reliable supply from Central Asia, China's top leaders have been strengthening relations with leadership from these regions and promoting bilateral and multilateral regional cooperation. In bilateral cooperation, China attaches importance to developing economic, trade, and security relations with countries in Central Asia and enhancing their oil security interests through the development of bilateral relations. Additionally, multilateral cooperation aims for regional economic and security integration in the framework of the SCO.

China and Central Asia Energy Cooperation

As energy cooperation progresses with official support, China and Central Asia have by now preliminarily established a structured cooperation mechanism that involves joint energy projects in both bilateral and multilateral approaches. Since the introduction of the 'going-out' strategy in the 1990s, China has actively invested in and facilitated the development of international oil, and Central Asia is a key strategic area in this context.[4] Chinese NOCs have been performing actively in upstream mergers and acquisitions and building supply infrastructure networks. The primary task is to expand China's upstream asset portfolio in the region as a way to diversify supply.

A historical review

China has actively participated in exploring and developing upstream resources in Central Asia, especially in Kazakhstan, Uzbekistan, and Turkmenistan, with NOCs such as CNPC as the key players. In June 1997, CNPC and the Kazakhstan government signed an agreement for the equity

---

4. Xuxin Wu, '经济全球化下中亚石油国际合作和中国石油国际合作之比较' [Comparison between Sino–Central Asian oil cooperation with China's international oil cooperation under the globalized economy], *Journal of Shengli Oilfield Party School* 19, no. 1 (2006): 101–103.

acquisition of AktobeMunaiGas.⁵ It obtained a 20-year user licence for the Zhanazhol gas site and the Kenkiyak oil site. Since then, China has made a number of upstream acquisitions in Kazakhstan. CNPC acquired stakes in the Salejan field and Aktyubinsk field in 2002 and 2003, respectively.⁶ China also attempted to compete with other upstream players in the region. In 2003, CNPC acquired the North Buzachi oil and gas field from the Nimir Petroleum Company and Chevron.⁷ This acquisition marked the first overseas oil field that was 100% owned by CNPC.

In late 2007, CNPC signed an agreement with KazMunayGas to export gas annually to China. Both parties confirmed the construction of the Kazakhstan-China gas pipeline, which became a part of the great Sino–Central Asia gas pipeline.⁸ In April 2009, CNPC and KazMunayGas purchased MangistauMunaiGas for US$3.3 billion and eventually acquired the entire company.⁹ CNPC was not the only active Chinese player in Kazakhstan. In 2004, Sinopec acquired the American First International Oil Company for around US$160 million, allowing the NOC to access the user licences of small fields such as Begaidar, Fedorov, Mezhdurechensk, Sagiz, and Sazankurak.¹⁰

Chinese NOC's energy investment was also active in other Central Asian countries. In 2006, Turkmenistan signed an energy agreement with China for the delivery of 30 bcm of Turkmen gas to China in 2009.¹¹ CNPC further signed a production agreement in 2007 in the Bagtyyarlyk field in Eastern Turkmenistan as well as a development contract in Turkmenistan's South Yolotan onshore gas field.¹² During former Chinese President Hu's visit to Uzbekistan in 2004, CNPC and Uzbekneftegaz signed several oil and gas contracts. Later in 2006, the two state-owned companies signed an oil and gas exploration agreement whereby CNPC was set to drill twenty-seven exploration wells in the country.¹³ Additionally, in 2005, Sinopec established a joint venture with the Ukrainian national oil and gas company to collaborate on

5. CNPC. 'CNPC in Kazakhstan', accessed 3 March 2012, http://classic.cnpc.com.cn/en/cnpcworldwide/kazakhstan.
6. Stephen J. Blank, 'China, Kazakh Energy and Russia: An Unlikely Ménage à Trois', *China and Eurasia Forum Quarterly* 3, no. 3 (2005): 99–109, 103; CNPC, 'CNPC in Kazakhstan', CNPC, 2008.
7. Energy Intelligence, 'Major Target: Chinese Set Their Sights on Kazakhstan', *Energy Intelligence*, 21 July 2003, https://www.energyintel.com/0000017b-a7a1-de4c-a17b-e7e331280001.
8. Sébastien Peyrouse, 'Central Asia's growing partnership with China' (Working Paper, EUCAM, 2008).
9. John Seaman, *Energy Security, Transnational Pipelines and China's Role in Asia* (Paris: Institut Français des Relations Internationales, 2010), 24.
10. Sébastien Peyrouse, 'Economic Aspects of the Chinese–Central Asia Rapprochement' (Working Paper, Central Asia–Caucasus Institute & Silk Road Studies Program, 2007).
11. Sébastien Peyrouse, 'Central Asia's Growing Partnership with China' (Working Paper, EUCAM, 2008).
12. John Seaman, *Energy Security, Transnational Pipelines and China's Role in Asia* (Paris: Institut Français des Relations Internationales, 2010).
13. Ramakant Dwivedi, 'China's Central Asia Policy in Recent Times', *China and Eurasia Forum Quarterly* 4, no. 4 (2006): 145–157, 148.

the exploration and development of the Andizhan oil field in Uzbekistan.[14] In 2008, the two companies further signed a cooperation agreement to develop a joint venture in the Mingbulak oil field.[15]

Transnational pipelines in China–Central Asia energy cooperation

Transnational oil and gas pipelines are a cornerstone in the China–Central Asia energy cooperation. Key pipeline projects include the construction of the Kazakhstan-China oil pipeline and the Central Asia–China gas pipeline.

Kazakhstan-China oil pipeline

The Kazakhstan-China oil pipeline was jointly developed by CNPC and the Kazakh oil company, KazMunayGas.[16] The current capacity of the pipeline is 14 million tonnes per year, and it reached a nominal capacity of 20 million tonnes per year in 2014.[17] The idea of an oil pipeline between Kazakhstan and China was conceptualised in 1993 and was agreed upon by CNPC and KazMunayGas in 1997 when both parties engaged in energy cooperation. The two parties signed a memorandum of understanding to build an eastward oil pipeline to China with an estimated cost of US$3.5 billion. China postponed construction due to price issues and competition from the Baku-Tbilisi-Ceyhan project. Yet, the first visit of former Chinese President Hu Jintao to Kazakhstan in June 2003 renewed China's momentum in building the pipeline[18] owing to the increase in Kazakhstan's oil production, an increase in oil prices worldwide, and the Angarsk failure.

Starting in September 2004, this 2,228-km-long pipeline stretches from the oil city of Atyrau in the western part of Kazakhstan to Alashankou in China's Xinjiang Province, at the border of the two countries.[19] The Kazakhstan-China oil pipeline is supplied from the Aktobe region's oil fields and Kashagan field

---

14. OGJ, 'Russian-Chinese Competition May Marginalize US, European Influence', *Oil and Gas Journal*, 13 March 2006, http://www.ogj.com/articles/print/volume-104/issue-10/exploration-development/central-asia-oil-and-gas-2-russian-chinese-competition-may-marginalize-us-european-influence.html.
15. Anne Marie Roantree, 'CNPC, Uzbekistan Tie Up to Develop Mingbulak Oilfield', *Reuters*, 20 October 2008.
16. Xinhua News, 'Kazakhstan-China Oil Pipeline Opens to Operation', *Xinhua News*, 12 July 2008.
17. Cecilia Rehn, 'Kazakhstan-China oil Pipeline Could Start Operating at Its Full Capacity by 2014', *Energy Global*, 9 November 2012.
18. Susann Handke, 'Securing and Fuelling China's Ascent to Power—The Geopolitics of the Chinese-Kazakh Oil Pipeline' (Working paper, Clingendael Institute of International Relations, 2006), 43–44.
19. Xinhua News, 'Kazakhstan-China Oil Pipeline Opens to Operation', *Xinhua News*, 12 July 2008.

in Kazakhstan.[20] The first phase of the Kenkiyak-Atyrau pipeline, originally in Kazakhstan, was officially put into operation in March 2003, covering a length of 448 km and the design stipulating an oil transportation capacity of 6 million tonnes per year. The second phase of the Atasu-Alashankou pipeline connecting China's Xinjiang Province began in September 2004, and was put into commercial operation in July 2006, covering 965 km, with the design stipulating an oil transportation capacity of 10 million tonnes per year. The third phase of the Kenkiyak-Atasu pipeline was constructed in May 2008 and put into commercial operation in October 2009, covering a length of 1,344 km, with the design stipulating an oil transportation capacity of 10 million tonnes per year.[21]

These projects were built and are operated jointly by both Chinese and Kazakh parties. The Atasu-Alashankou section of the pipeline, which is near the Chinese-Kazakh border, is operated by MunaiTas, a joint venture between CNPC and KazMunayGas.[22] The Kenkiyak-Kumkol section in the Kazakh territory was built and is operated by a joint venture between China National Oil and Gas Exploration and Development Corporation (CNODC) and KazTransOil JSC.[23] At the Chinese end, the Kazakhstan-China oil pipeline is connected to the Dushanzi District in Xinjiang Province of China via the Alashankou-Dushanzi crude oil pipeline.

Central Asia–China gas pipeline

The Central Asia–China gas pipeline is China's largest overseas natural gas project, involving four sections of pipeline infrastructures in four countries: China, Kazakhstan, Uzbekistan, and Turkmenistan. China initiated the project in the early 2000s with offers of infrastructure development and loans with low interest rates.[24] The initial proposal for this pipeline was presented as the Kazakhstan-China gas pipeline when the agreement was signed in June 2003, when China's President Hu Jintao visited Kazakhstan.[25] The CNPC-KazMunayGaz partnership planned to start the construction of the

---

20. Alexander Sukhanov, 'Caspian Oil Exports Heading East', *Asian Times*, 9 February 2005.
21. Sébastien Peyrouse, 'Central Asia's Growing Partnership with China' (Working Paper, EUCAM, 2008); Cunhui Li, '中哈原油管道合作双赢开辟能源通道' [Win-Win Situation in Sino-Kazakhstan oil pipeline open energy corridor], *China Petroleum Daily*, 17 December 2010.
22. People's Daily, 'Kazakhstan-China oil Pipeline to Open in May', *People's Daily Online*, 27 February 2006.
23. Maria Golovnina, 'Kazakhstan, China Agree on Pipeline from Caspian', *Reuters*, 18 August 2007.
24. Keunwook Paik, Marcel Valerie, Lahn Glada, John V. Mitchell, and Erkin Adylov, 'Trends in Asian National Oil Company Investments Abroad: An Update' (Working Paper, Chatham House, 2007), http://www.chathamhouse.org.uk/files/6427_r0307anoc.pdf.
25. China Daily, 'China, Kazakhstan Discuss Cross-Border Gas Pipeline', *China Daily*, 25 August 2004.

Kazakhstan natural gas pipeline in 2008, following the Kazakhstan-China oil pipeline. This transnational pipeline project between Kazakhstan and China laid the foundation for expanding the pipeline network to other Central Asian countries, including Turkmenistan.

In 2006, China and Turkmenistan signed a framework agreement on pipeline construction and long-term gas supply.[26] A year later, the two parties announced that Turkmenistan was joining the Kazakhstan-China gas pipeline, and a transnational gas pipeline would thus be built to export natural gas to China.[27] Although the energy cooperation between China and Turkmenistan started late, it developed very quickly. In the same year, China and Uzbekistan signed an agreement on the construction and exploitation of the pipeline's Uzbek section,[28] with operations starting in mid-2008.

The Kazakh section of the pipeline was inaugurated in late 2009 during former President Hu Jintao's visit to Kazakhstan,[29] with the leaders of Turkmenistan, Uzbekistan, and Kazakhstan. Later in 2010, China and Kazakhstan signed an agreement on an additional branch line to China from Western Kazakhstan.[30] Initially, the Central Asia–China gas pipeline had dual parallel lines, Line A and Line B (with Line C and D expanding at a later stage), each running for 1,833 km. It starts at the Turkmen-Uzbek border and runs through central Uzbekistan and southern Kazakhstan before reaching China's northwest region of Xinjiang, following the Turkmenistan-Uzbekistan-Kazakhstan-Erdos-Urumqi-Lanzhou-Xian-Shanghai route. Line A became operational in late 2009, and Line B started running in 2010.[31]

According to the initial sales and purchase agreement between CNPC and Turkmengaz, which was signed in 2007, China would receive 30 bcm of Turkmen gas annually via Lines A and B for 30 years, with 13 bcm of natural gas annually from the Amu Darya project, and 17 bcm of natural gas annually from Turkmengaz State Concern.[32] In 2012, construction began for Line C of the pipeline, parallel to A and B, and this line was designed to deliver 25 bcm gas annually to China. Line C is supplied by 10 bcm, 10 bcm, and 5 bcm of natural gas per year from Turkmenistan, Uzbekistan, and Kazakhstan, respectively.[33] The construction of the fourth pipeline, Line D, started in 2014. It is

---

26. Forbes, 'Turkmenistan to Join China, Kazakhstan Pipeline Project—KazMunaiGas EP CEO', *Forbes AFX News*, 4 July 2007.
27. Daniel Kimmage, 'Central Asia: Turkmenistan-China Pipeline Project Has Far-Reaching Implications', *Radio Free Europe/Radio Liberty*, 10 April 2006.
28. CNPC, 'Central Asia-China Gas Pipeline', CNPC, http://www.cnpc.com.cn/en/CentralAsia/CentralAsia_index.shtml.
29. Raushan Nurshayeva and Shamil Zhumatov, 'China's Hu Boosts Energy Ties with Central Asia', *Reuters*, 12 December 2009.
30. Zhihong Wan, 'China, Kazakhstan Sign New Gas Pipeline Deal', *China Daily*, 14 June 2010.
31. CNPC, 'Central Asia–China Gas Pipeline', CNPC, 2010, https://www.cnpc.com.cn/en/CentralAsia/CentralAsia_index.shtml.
32. CNPC, 'Flow of Natural Gas from Central Asia', CNPC, 2013, http://www.cnpc.com.cn/en/FlowofnaturalgasfromCentralAsia/FlowofnaturalgasfromCentralAsia2.shtml.
33. Ibid.

expected to transport gas from the Galkynysh gas field in Turkmenistan and be routed via Uzbekistan, Tajikistan, and Kyrgyzstan to China.[34]

The Central Asia–China gas pipeline is China's first and largest cross-border gas pipeline. According to CNPC, all four lines of the pipeline network will be able to supply China with 85 bcm of gas yearly, accounting for at least 40% of China's total imported gas supplies in the next three decades.[35] Aside from fostering economic cooperation between China and Central Asian countries, the pipeline has also become a source of prosperity for the region, promoting the development of and investment in local natural gas resources, stimulating the growth of local equipment manufacturing and construction industries, and creating employment opportunities.

These China–Central Asia pipelines are all connected to China's domestic gas pipeline network, the West-East Gas Pipeline, with the farthest scope to the Yangtze River Delta, Pearl River Delta, and Hong Kong and Macao. In summary, the construction of transnational oil and gas pipelines for China is very consistent with the strategic considerations of energy security and reduced dependence on sea transport modes. With a total length of almost 10,000 km, the natural gas pipeline connecting the two countries passes through Turkmenistan, Uzbekistan, Kazakhstan, and China, ranking as the world's longest natural gas pipeline.

Energy cooperation with Central Asia has not always been easy for China. For example, China failed in its bid for British Gas's stake in the Agip KCO International Consortium in 2005 because Chinese NOCs were not included in major consortiums of international majors, such as ConocoPhillips, ExxonMobil, Shell, and TotalFinaElf.[36] Therefore, the aforementioned acquisitions and projects were considered a breakthrough for Chinese companies in their overseas oil and gas exploration. In short, energy cooperation between China and Central Asian countries has been broadening and deepening with the following characteristics:[37]

- The cooperation is not only limited to trade but also includes investment.
- The scope has expanded from upstream development (i.e., exploration and production) to midstream and downstream participation (i.e., transport, storage, and supply networks).
- There is growing all-round technical cooperation covering all areas, including production, transportation, storage, and resource utilisation.

---

34. Ibid.
35. Ibid.
36. Irina Ionela Pop, 'China's Energy Strategy in Central Asia: Interactions with Russia, India and Japan', UNISCI Discussion Papers 24 (2010): 197–220.
37. Keunwook Paik, senior fellow at Chatham House, interview with the author, 2018; Yishan Xia, senior fellow at the China Institute of International Studies, interview with the author, 2021.

- There is increasing Chinese involvement in the Central Asian upstream sector.
- The active participation of Central Asian companies has quickened the implementation of projects, especially at the initial stage of work, such as feasibility studies.
- Investment in large-scale infrastructure, particularly transnational pipelines, is always a part of cooperation.

In order to achieve its policy goal on energy security, Chinese authorities and national companies have adopted a variety of instruments and models for its energy cooperation with Central Asian countries, including the production-sharing model, joint management model, and technology service model.

1. Production-sharing model

The production sharing model is based on the premise that governments have ownership and franchise of oil and gas resources, and foreign oil and gas companies are responsible for the exploration, development, and production costs. When it is time to use the resources, these companies negotiate and sign oil and gas exploration and development contracts on how to share products with the resource-owning governments (or oil and gas companies of such countries).

Most terms of this model can be fulfilled through consultations between the two cooperative sides. The main terms include national participation, signing fees, and various taxes, such as production bonus, mining royalty, and income tax. The core items are the fiscal and taxation costs related to cost recovery and production sharing. The actual operation of this model in the oil and gas fields in Central Asia is primarily through the direct investment of foreign oil and gas companies, the establishment of consortiums with oil and gas companies of resource-owning countries, the signing of production-sharing agreements, and participation in the development of one or more projects.

2. Joint management model

The joint management model can be divided into two categories: the joint venture model and joint operation model. In joint ventures, national oil and gas companies of resource-owning countries and contractors fund and set up a new company according to a certain pre-agreed percentage. As an independent legal entity, the new company is engaged in oil and gas exploration, development, production, transportation, and sales, and the two sides bear the risk of operation, share tax liability, and share the revenue according to the proportions stated in the contract.[38] Meanwhile, in the joint operation model, the two sides do not need to form joint venture companies, but they operate and share

---

38. Ibid.

risk and revenue together as per the joint operation agreement they have. This model is widely applied in the practice of oil and gas resource development in Central Asia. Additionally, the tax system is adjusted through the mineral tax, and the main categories of taxes include corporate income tax, dividend tax, value-added tax, income tax of non-foreign nationals, tax for developing mineral resources, crude oil export income tax, excess profit tax, etc.

3. Technology service model

The technology service model, refers to the cooperation by which a party takes their technological knowledge as the carrier to solve specific technical problems for the other party. In this model, when the investing country and resource-owning country collaborate to develop resources, advanced technology support is provided, advanced management experience is brought, and the infrastructure needed to develop resources is improved.

These three cooperation models are crucial to the China–Central Asia cooperation, as they solve the two main obstacles characterising it and can result in a structural transformation in terms of how China approaches Central Asia regarding energy issues. First, the models reduce the trade barriers regarding taxes and provide technological development for the infrastructure linking the two sides, such as transportation pipelines. Joint management can also facilitate cooperation between China and other countries in the region. As a result of the cooperation undertaken by the countries under these models over time, the groundwork was well established for the initial proposal of transnational oil and gas pipelines from Kazakhstan to China in 2003.[39]

China's Energy Diplomacy in Central Asia

While Central Asian countries are China's key targets in its energy diplomacy strategy, the Chinese government supports the investment of its NOCs in Central Asia bilaterally and multilaterally in at least four ways.

Frequent state visits

In energy diplomacy, relevant diplomatic meetings are always used to promote the signing of energy cooperation agreements. Chinese leaders pay frequent visits to Central Asian countries, and the exchange between high-level officials has backed up various energy deals as part of the 'energy partnership' agreement between the leaderships. The parties have also arranged high-level meetings to discuss energy issues. In 1994, when economic ties between China and Central Asia were marginal, former Premier Li Peng visited Turkmenistan and promoted cooperation between CNPC and the Turkmen Ministry of Oil

---

39. Ibid.

and Natural Gas.[40] In 1996, former President Jiang Zemin visited Kazakhstan, and soon afterwards in the following year, CNPC started its footprint in Kazakhstan and reached an agreement on the cross-border oil pipeline from Kazakhstan to China.[41]

When former President Hu made his first state visit to Kazakhstan in 2003, China and Kazakhstan issued a joint statement announcing the strengthening of oil and natural gas cooperation and signed an agreement to jointly develop the China-Kazakhstan oil pipeline.[42] In return, when Kazakhstan's former President Nazarbayev visited China in February 2011, the two countries again signed several agreements on energy cooperation, including a loan agreement between the Development Bank of Kazakhstan and the Export-Import Bank of China on a joint infrastructure construction, an agreement in principle between KazMunaiGaz and CNPC the Urikhtau energy project, and a framework agreement between Kazphosphate and Sinochem on strategic cooperation.[43] Notably, the vision of the BRI was first articulated by Chinese President Xi during his visit to Kazakhstan in September 2013, reflecting the importance of Central Asia to the Initiative.

Promotion of bilateral economic and trade relations

As seen from the trade structure between China and Central Asia, the two sides have strongly complemented each other economically, which in turn guarantees a favourable environment for energy trade. China attaches great importance to friendly cooperation with Central Asian countries. Together, they have signed plenty of intergovernmental cooperation agreements in the fields of energy, economy and trade, culture and education, and so on. Regarding energy, China and Central Asian countries have already signed some guiding agreements in the form of joint declarations, intergovernmental economic and trade agreements, and other agreements that concern concessional loans and investment in energy.

In 1994, when Premier Li Peng visited four countries in Central Asia, he also proposed six points underpinning the bilateral economic and trade

---

40. PRC MFA, 'Bilateral Relationship between China and Turkmenistan', PRC MFA, 2007, http://www.mfa.gov.cn/chn/wjb/zzjg/dozys/gjlb/1781/default.htm.
41. 'Philip Andrews-Speed, *The Strategic Implications of China's Energy Needs* (London: Routledge, 2014), 59.
42. China Daily, 'China, Kazakhstan Discuss Cross-Border Gas Pipeline', *China Daily*, 25 August 2004.
43. Leslie Hook, 'Kazakhstan Embraces Chinese Investment', *Financial Times*, 22 February 2011; Jacqueline Wong, 'KazMunaiGas in Deal to Tap Urikhtau Gas Field', *Reuters*, 23 February 2011; PRC SASAC, '中化集团与哈萨克磷公司签署战略合作框架协议' [Sinochem signed framework agreement with KPC], PRC SASAC, 2011, http://www.sasac.gov.cn/n86114/n326638/c958714/content.html.

relations between the two sides:[44] (1) adhere to equality and mutual interest principles and follow the economic principles; (2) diversify forms of cooperation; (3) make optimal use of local resources; (4) improve transport conditions and construct the 'New Silk Road'; (5) provide financial assistance to the Central Asian countries; and (6) develop multilateral cooperation and promote common development. Since then, Central Asian countries have increased exports to China,[45] such as energy (Kazakhstan, Turkmenistan, and Uzbekistan), metals (Kazakhstan and Kyrgyzstan), and textiles (Kyrgyzstan, Turkmenistan, and Uzbekistan). Energy trade with Central Asian countries also becomes an important backbone of the 'going-out' strategy and BRI.

Multilateral platforms

Although China traditionally takes a bilateral approach in its energy investments in Central Asia, it is also involved in multilateral platforms such as the SCO to develop mutual trust with other Central Asian countries and maintain its influence in the region: 'The purposes of the SCO are: strengthening mutual trust and good-neighbourly friendship among the member states; encouraging effective cooperation among the member states in political, economic and trade, scientific and technological, cultural, educational, energy, communications, environment and other fields; devoting themselves jointly to preserving and safeguarding regional peace, security and stability; and establishing a democratic, fair and rational new international political and economic order'.[46] The member states also set up the SCO Energy Club to promote energy cooperation under the organisation. These mechanisms for strengthening China's role in global energy governance were carried into the BRI.

Chinese Energy Cooperation via the SCO

The SCO is a Eurasian political, economic, and military organisation that was founded in 2001 in Shanghai by the leaders of China, Kazakhstan, Kyrgyzstan, Russia, Tajikistan, and Uzbekistan. The Shanghai Five grouping, which was originally created in 1996 by the membership of Uzbekistan and the signing of the Treaty on Deepening Military Trust in Border Regions, was transformed to create the SCO. It is primarily centred on its member nations' security-related concerns in Central Asia in terms of terrorism, separatism, and extremism.

---

44. People's Daily, 'Premier Li Peng Put Forward Six Proposals on Economic and Trade Cooperation between China and Central Asian Countries', *People's Daily*, 27 April 1994.
45. Vladimir Paramonov, 'China and Central Asia: Present and Future of Economic Relations' (Working Paper, Conflict Studies Research Centre, 2005).
46. SCO, 'Declaration on Establishment of SCO', Shanghai Cooperation Organisation, 2006, http://english.scosummit2006.org/en_bjzl/2006-04/20/content_85.htm.

David Kerr identifies the three aims of the SCO as 'repressing transnational radicalism; stabilising regional regimes and their foreign policy orientations; and checking US influence'.[47] Since the SCO was founded in 2001, its activities in the social development of its member states have increased rapidly. Both energy cooperation and that in other areas of common interest—such as politics, trade, national defence, law enforcement, environmental conservation, culture, technology, education, traffic, financial credit, and so on—generally have three stages: improving the cooperation mechanism, laying down the principles and strategies of cooperation, and consolidating the basis of cooperation through projects. The Eurasian organisation has been widely criticised by external observers as an 'OPEC' with nuclear power,[48] and a prospective 'Asian NATO' against the US.[49] The organisation is also considered an ineffectual and shallow regional 'talk-fest' or a transparent cloak for the maintenance and expansion of malignant Chinese influence in Central Asia.[50]

However, these observations fail to fully address the functions of the SCO and the core imperatives of one of its key members—China. The underlying rationale of Chinese energy cooperation via the SCO is similar to that of antiterrorism. China realised that it had to enhance energy security in the region and reach an agreement in border areas of common interests. It did the same for anti-terrorism via the 1998 joint statement, declaring that the member states would not 'allow their territories to be used for activities undermining the national sovereignty, security, and social order of any of the five countries'.[51] This document also contained the 'concrete manifestation of the new-type security concept' and emphasised the pursuit of common interests, peaceful dialogue, common security for all regional actors, and the discouragement of formal hierarchical alliances.[52] This had become a dominant trope in China's foreign policy discourse and applied to its energy agenda underlying its involvement in SCO. In a nutshell, China's foreign policy in Central Asia is important for China's energy security, and China's westward advance into Central Asia is also determined by its growing need for energy resources.

Energy cooperation has been frequently addressed in SCO meetings over the last two decades. In September 2003, the second Prime Ministers' Meeting

---

47. David Kerr Laura C. Swinton, 'China, Xinjiang and the Transnational Security of Central Asia', *Critical Asian Studies* 40, no. 1 (2008): 89–112.
48. Matthew Brummer, 'The Shanghai Cooperation Organization and Iran: A Power-Full Union', *Journal of International Affairs* 60, no. 2 (2007): 185–198, 185.
49. Richard Weitz, 'Shanghai Summit Fails to Yield NATO-Style Defence Agreement', *Jane's Intelligence Review* 18, no. 8 (2006): 40–43.
50. Stephen Blank, 'China's Defeats in Central Asia', *Central Asia-Caucasus Analyst*, 14 August 2002; Simon Tisdall, 'Irresistible Rise of the Dictators' Club', *The Guardian*, 6 June 2006.
51. People's Daily, '中、塔、俄、哈、吉五国《杜尚别声明》' [China, Tajikistan, Russia, Kazakhstan, and Kyrgyzstan signed the Dushanbe Declaration], *People's Daily*, 5 July 2000.
52. Marc Lanteigne, *China and International Institutions: Alternate Paths to Global Power* (London: Routledge, 2005).

of SCO member countries in Beijing approved the Outline of Multilateral Economic and Trade Cooperation among SCO members, indicating that regional economic cooperation, including energy ones, was gradually getting back on track.[53] A year later, the third Economic and Trade Ministers' Meeting in Moscow led to an agreement on the Outline of Multilateral Economic and Trade Cooperation among the SCO countries, which included eleven areas and 127 projects in energy.[54] In 2006, the Economic and Trade Ministers' Meeting in Tashkent resulted in consensus on setting up a professional working group that aimed to promote cooperation. In the same year, Russian President Vladimir Putin delivered a speech at the sixth Meeting of the Council of Heads of State of the SCO, where he pointed out that 'the SCO has a sufficient organisational and legal infrastructure to actively engage in promising economic projects' and 'the proposal to create an SCO Energy Club is a topical one, as well as expanding cooperation in transport and communications'.[55]

As a follow-up move, on 29 June 2007, the SCO Energy Ministers' Meeting in Moscow emphasised the necessity of close cooperation. The meeting reviewed common ground and disagreement in energy cooperation among SCO member states. At the same time, during the meeting, former Russian Prime Minister Zubkov suggested that SCO member countries should actively prepare for the SCO Energy Club, highlighting energy cooperation as one of the most important tasks of the organisation.[56] On 16 August 2007, an SCO council meeting further pointed out that economic cooperation within the framework had entered the implementation stage, in which relevant plans and agreements are carried out in multiple areas in energy, traffic, telecommunication, etc. with derived benefits.[57] The importance of close coordination among SCO member countries and SCO industrial committees and bank associations was also emphasised during the meeting. On 28 August 2008, the eighth SCO council meeting in Dushanbe welcomed 'the positive dynamics which had appeared in a number of areas of common interest in trade and economic cooperation' and emphasised 'the creation of favourable trade and investment conditions, development of transportation routes and transit potential, modern information and telecommunication technologies'.[58] It

---

53. PRC MFA, '上海合作组织成员国总理会议' [Shanghai Cooperation Organization (SCO) meeting], PRC MFA, 2013, http://www.fmprc.gov.cn/mfa_chn/wjb_602314/zzjg_602420/dozys_602828/dqzzoys_602832/shhz_602834_1/gk_602836.
54. Ibid.
55. Vladimir Putin, 'Speech at the Shanghai Cooperation Organisation Council of Heads of State', Kremlin, 2006, http://en.kremlin.ru/events/president/transcripts/23643.
56. Sergei Blagov, 'Russia Urges Formation of Central Asian Energy Club', *Eurasianet*, 7 November 2007.
57. PRC MFA, 'Joint Communique of Meeting of Council of Heads of SCO Members', PRC MFA, 2013, http://www.fmprc.gov.cn/mfa_eng/wjdt_665385/2649_665393/t355665.shtml.
58. PRC MFA, 'Dushanbe Declaration of Heads of SCO Member States', PRC MFA, 2008, https://www.mfa.gov.cn/ce/cgsf//eng/xw/t513027.htm.

stressed that the energy mechanism of the SCO should be based on the principles of openness with countries and organisations that agree with its purposes and tasks. Later in October, a prime minister's meeting in Astana witnessed a pledge to implement the consensus reached at Dushanbe to promote the sustainable development of multilateral cooperation within the SCO. They agreed to deepen multilateral economic and trade cooperation and boost cooperation in 'enhancing energy efficiency, developing clean energy, utilising renewable energy, and ensuring energy security.[59]

With guidance from the heads of state and governments of member countries, SCO energy cooperation has been implemented by relevant departments and enterprises. While the organisation has achieved a lot in promoting high-level energy cooperation in the last decade, the policy suggestions made in these meetings indicate a conceptual change to promote energy cooperation multilaterally. In October 2009, the eighth SCO Prime Ministers' meeting agreed to work out measures to increase multilateral economic cooperation. Additionally, China proposed to enhance regional cooperation with the construction of infrastructures, including energy projects.[60] The joint decision to implement a range of joint projects reflected a materialisation of energy cooperation via SCO. These mechanisms were further incorporated into the BRI framework, with a broader scope of cooperation.

The above examples of SCO energy cooperation indicate that geographic position, policy framework and pre-existing logistic network are key factors facilitating energy investments and trade in/with Central Asia. The complement of energy projects promotes the development of the economy and transportation, infrastructure construction, structure of energy consumption, and improvement of living standards in all member countries. Involved countries have realised that only energy cooperation based on mutual benefits can meet the fundamental interests of each country.

Multilateralism in China–Central Asia Energy Cooperation

Multiple high-level SCO meetings have indicated that China and other SCO member states have attempted to establish a regional mechanism to address transnational energy investment and transit issues, especially after the start of the China–Central Asia transnational pipeline. Since 2004, the Council of Heads of State of the SCO, which includes China, has repeatedly stated that the SCO would prioritise energy cooperation within the SCO framework.[61] To promote economic and trade cooperation, an energy working group on

---

59. PRC MFA, 'SCO Prime Ministers Discuss Cooperation in Astana', PRC MFA, 2008, http://www.china-embassy.org/eng/ywzn/lsyw/oca/200810/t20081030_4904545.htm.
60. PRC MFA, 'The Eighth SCO Prime Ministers' Meeting Is Held in Beijing Wen Jiabao Chairs the Meeting', PRC MFA, 2009, https://www.mfa.gov.cn/ce/cgsf//eng/xw/t620813.htm.
61. Guangcheng Xing, 上海合作组织发展报告2009 [Shanghai Cooperation Organization Development Report 2009] (Beijing: CASS Publishing).

modern information and telecommunications technology was established within the framework of the organisation. In particular, Russian President Putin's proposal of 'Energy Club' in 2006 was well-received by all other member countries. China and other SCO member states have also tried to implement and promote a variety of energy cooperation programmes via the SCO under the Measurement Plan of the Outline of Multilateral Economy and Trade Cooperation.

However, the actual implementation of energy projects among SCO member states mostly remained bilateral, such as agreement and coordination between governments or companies, and did not always rely on SCO's multilateral framework. For example, the SCO was not considered as a major platform for China and Central Asian countries to coordinate or manage key projects such as transnational pipelines. This is the result of limited legal mechanisms in the SCO rather than a lack of willingness to take the multilateral approach. Moreover, also long as bilateral solutions were working, there was no great urgency for China to look into a new legal or coordination mechanism.

Energy cooperation, particularly transnational pipeline management, could be a rather complicated legal issue, involving transit regulation, different energy laws among different countries, and huge financial transactions.[62] Ideally, SCO can serve as an important regional organisation that provides the legal framework for regional energy cooperation but there are multiple constraining factors. David Kerr argues that the regional problem of China and the unclear future of the SCO results in a fluid environment for energy cooperation in Central Asia.[63] Historical issues, security concerns, domestic problems, great power competition, and a growing number of investors, were ongoing challenges for China's multilateral engagement via SCO in the region.[64]

The implementation of China–Central Asian transnational pipeline has painted a different picture as it has structurally changed the dynamics of how China approaches Central Asian countries. By constructing a transnational infrastructure, it has effectively created long-term interdependencies among multiple actors, including suppliers, consumers, and transit countries. The significant amount of funds invested means that it is difficult and expensive for any country to quit the partnership. Long-term gas supply contracts have also led to long-term political ties. Sections of the pipeline are located in specific countries or regions, and once the line is confirmed, countries along it are physically tied to a network of infrastructures. Joint construction is a commitment from multiple parties to their long-term supply and demand,

---

62. A former officer from an international energy organisation, interview with the author, 2014.
63. David Kerr and Laura C. Swinton, 'China, Xinjiang and the Transnational Security of Central Asia', *Critical Asian Studies* 40, no. 1 (2008): 89–112.
64. Yishan Xia, senior fellow at the China Institute of International Studies, interview with the author, 2021.

and also reflects their willingness to establish an interdependent and mutually constraining partnership. This is also the reason why energy trade via the China–Central Asian transnational pipeline continues to be an important project in the BRI.[65]

Transnational pipelines do not only generate economic benefits, but also provide safety in terms of geopolitics. Moreover, such cooperation on pipeline construction can enhance political trust between the countries along the line, and an overflow effect can be created. The political stability and financial viability of China and Central Asia must be weighed and maintained in the context of broader international goals and multilateral platforms. It also increases the need to deal with cross-border energy investment and transit with a multilateral mechanism. In sum, the China–Central Asia cooperation via the transnational pipeline has paved the way for multilateralism.

China's growing presence in the region has also increased the need for investment protection provided by international organisations or treaties. While the bilateral approach could be more effective, investments will still need a certain degree of legal protection. A study by the Energy Charter Secretariat argues, 'As more and more Chinese energy investments flow into Eurasian countries, there is a potential risk that those investments might be blocked by unfair and/or discriminatory treatments imposed by the host countries. A certain amount of Chinese multilateral cooperative frameworks or mechanisms that exist in the Central Asian region are not legally binding. Thus far, political conciliation and diplomatic mediation are the most frequently used measures in case of energy investment disputes or transit interruptions.'[66]

Indeed, Chinese authorities and NOCs are aware of the potential investment risks and the need for treaty protection. For example, they recognised that the transit risks of a transnational pipeline could be potentially reduced by the Energy Charter Treaty (ECT).[67] However, since there has not been a major supply or transit crisis so far, China does not need to actively join or sign one. China would only turn to the ECT after it fully recognises that the treaty can reduce transit risks to its energy investment in the region but there is no immediate need. There is also a possibility for China to unpack the framework of these international organisations or treaties and establish a new energy cooperation mechanism of its own that allows the country to better coordinate with Central Asian countries.[68] Yet, that would require significant diplomatic effect, substantial financial resources, and years of time to achieve such a goal.

---

65. Ibid.
66. Zhuwei Wang, 'Securing Energy Flows from Central Asia to China: Relevance of the Energy Charter Treaty' (Brussel: Energy Charter Secretariat, 2014).
67. A former officer from an international energy organisation, interview with the author, 2014.
68. For example, the Belt and Road Initiative. See Chapter 3.

4
China-Africa Energy Cooperation

From Oil Diplomacy to Low-Carbon Investments

Traditionally, China's interest in African resources has been primarily driven by Beijing's desire to secure an upstream supply and its ambition to enhance intergovernmental collaboration between China and Africa. In the short term, China must secure oil supplies to feed its growing domestic economy, and in the long term, China aims to increase its influence over the global energy supply chain. David Zweig pointed out that China has linked its foreign policy to its domestic development initiatives via the going-out strategy to an unprecedented level by encouraging state-controlled companies to seek out exploration and supply contracts with commodity-producing countries.[1] China aims to strengthen oil cooperation with African countries and form closer ties, diversify energy supply sources to enhance energy security, and reduce oil dependence on the Middle East region. While China-African energy relationship has been defined by a combination of economic and political considerations, green development is also an emerging aspect in their cooperation as China and Africa recognise that climate change is one of the most serious challenges.

Mutual needs have paved the way for China-Africa energy cooperation. From China's going-out strategy to the BRI, Africa has been a major destination for Chinese investments. It is not surprising that Africa has turned into a major investment destination of Chinese energy companies in such a broad economic context.

---

1. David Zweig and Bi Jianhai, 'China's Global Hunt for Energy', *Foreign Affairs* 8, no. 5 (2005): 25–38.

China-Africa Energy Cooperation

The expansion of Chinese NOCs' footprint in Africa demonstrates the importance of the continent to energy security in China. The sectoral reform in China in the 1990s created new opportunities for NOCs to participate in overseas business. In 1993, under the national agenda to integrate industry and international trade, the China United Oil Company was jointly founded by the Ministry of Economy and Trade, CNPC, and China National Chemicals Import and Export Corporation. The integration was expected to enhance China's advantage in international competition, especially in overseas energy activities, such as the exploration, production, sales, import, and export of oil and natural gas resources.[2]

1. Cooperation in oil and gas

In the mid-1990s, CNPC started its oil journey in Sudan, which was regarded as an important breakthrough for Chinese global energy investment. Together with other international oil majors, it started to develop oil blocks in Sudan.[3] In the mid-2000s, China made further progress in its oil cooperation with Western Africa, particularly with Angola and Nigeria. Other than acquiring oil assets for new discoveries and production in these countries, Chinese NOCs also attempted to develop a new procurement pattern to purchase a stake in established companies.[4]

Chinese investment in African oil projects continued in the 2010s, especially in East Africa. In 2012, CNPC acquired a 28.57% stake in Eni East Africa, which held a 70% interest in the Area 4 gas block in offshore Mozambique before the deal.[5] CNPC secured its interest with US$4.21 billion to participate indirectly in the Mozambique Rovuma Basin, where Eni had discovered at least 75 trillion cubic feet of gas. Since then, there have been massive offshore gas discoveries in the Rovuma Basin in Mozambique, implying CNPC has created its footprint in one of the potentially largest LNG exporting countries. CNPC's entrance to Mozambique's LNG sector is strategically significant for extending Sino-African energy cooperation to a new domain. Following the new discovery and production of oil and gas in Africa, China is expected to increase its investment in the continent.[6]

---

2. Daojiong Zha, 'China's Energy Security: Domestic and International Issues', *Survival: Global Politics and Strategy* 48, no. 1 (2006): 179–190.
3. Jemera Rone, 'Sudan: Oil & War', *African Political Economy* 30, no. 97 (2003): 504–510.
4. Theodore H. Moran, *China's Strategy to Secure Natural Resources: Risks, Dangers, and Opportunities* (Washington: Peterson Institute for International Economics, 2010).
5. OGJ, 'CNPC Completes Buy of Stake off Mozambique', *Oil & Gas Journal*, 23 July 2013, http://www.ogj.com/articles/2013/07/cnpc-completes-buy-of-stake-off-mozambique.html.
6. David Ledesma, 'East Africa Gas—Potential for Export' (Report, Oxford Institute for Energy Studies, 2013).

2. Cooperation in critical minerals in clean energy transitions

As the largest producer of lithium cells, accounting for around 70% of the global manufacturing capacity, China seeks to find a stable source for low-cost cobalt by exploring deposits in Africa. The top-three African countries that have benefited from China's investments are Zambia, South Africa, and the Democratic Republic of Congo (DRC) because these countries have large, high-grade copper and cobalt deposits. For instance, since nearly 60% of cobalt ore is found in the DRC, Chinese enterprises have proactively invested in the cobalt mining industry in the DRC to guarantee stable access to cobalt resources.[7] In 2018, China formed a 35-member Union of Mining Companies with Chinese capital, which is supported by both the Chinese and DRC governments.[8] As a result of China's efforts, as of 2018, Chinese companies control around 24% of the total value of minerals and metals produced in the DRC.[9] Guinea, a major greenfield bauxite producer, has been strengthening commodity trade with China amid strong criticism from Brussels and Washington over President Condé's third term in office.[10]

3. Cooperation in renewable energy

Renewable energy is also an emerging area in Sino-African energy cooperation especially after the Paris Agreement in 2015. The continent faces both major challenges and massive opportunities for clean energy amid African governments' support for the energy transition.[11] The increasing demand for electricity for both industry and household consumption requires a major upgrade of the power system in Africa. Filling in the demand gap, in 2016, Chinese investment accounted for 30% of new power capacity in sub-Saharan Africa, with over half of them in renewable energy, such as wind, solar, and hydropower.[12] Chinese investment in renewable energy in African continued to growing in the following years and potential co-benefits generated from

---

7. Research and Markets, 'Global and China Cobalt Industry Report, 2018–2023' (Report, Research and Markets, 2019).
8. William Clowes, 'China Marks Cobalt, Copper Ascendancy in Congo with New Group', *Bloomberg*, 18 June 2018, https://www.bloomberg.com/news/articles/2018-06-18/china-marks- cobalt-copper-ascendancy-in-congo-with-new-group.
9. Magnus Ericsson, Olof Löf, and Anton Löf, 'Chinese Control over African and Global Mining—Past, Present and Future', *Mineral Economics* 33, no. 1 (2020): 153-181.
10. BBC, 'Guinea Elections: Alpha Condé Wins Third Term amid Violent Protests', *BBC*, 24 October 2020, https://www.bbc.com/news/world-africa-54657359.
11. IEA, 'Africa Faces Both Major Challenges and Huge Opportunities as It Transitions to Clean Energy', IEA, 2022, https://www.iea.org/news/africa-faces-both-major-challenges-and-huge-opportunities-as-it-transitions-to-clean-energy.
12. IEA, 'Boosting the Power Sector in Sub-Saharan Africa: China's Involvement: International Energy Agency', IEA, 2016, https://www.iea.org/publications/freepublications/publication/Partner_Country_SeriesChinaBoosting_the_Power_Sector_in_SubSaharan_Africa_Chinas_Involvement.pdf.

these projects remain a key factor that drives the Chinese and African governments to advance their cooperation.[13]

A common characteristic of Chinese investment in Africa is resource-backed development loans, in which China offers loans or infrastructure construction services in exchange for natural resources. For example, in 2002, when Angola experienced severe economic development difficulties, China first offered a commercial loan for public services, which was to be repaid with oil, and also signed a framework agreement with the country. China has been providing diverse types of aid attached to its investment in Africa.[14] China considers this as a way of supporting Africa's economic development, as well as strengthening economic and trade ties. This promotes the economic development of the recipient countries and alleviates the pressure of China's oil shortage. In short, providing aid to Africa, directly or indirectly, promotes the economic development of African countries and keeps China's oil supply stable.

China's advantages in energy investments in Africa

From the going-out strategy to the BRI, Chinese NOCs have been expanding their upstream asset portfolio in Africa via mergers and acquisitions, joint ventures, trade, and investment. China has become a major competitor of other Western countries in Africa with at least three advantages.

First, Chinese investors are generally welcomed in Africa because of their flexible loan requirements compared to Western creditors, which are more concerned with social and environmental compliance. Western investors are obligated to operate with tighter international benchmarks related to environmental damage, business transparency, and human rights. In contrast, Chinese investors face far less scrutiny on these issues, presenting a greater appeal to operate in high-risk areas. Moreover, since Chinese overseas investments always follow the concept of non-interference in domestic affairs, there are less political conditions in their business contracts.[15]

Second, African countries could consider Chinese investors as an alternative to Western ones. Edinger indicated that 'China's approach in terms of development assistance is one of mutual respect where even smaller African countries, with little economic or political significance will receive both aid

---

13. Rasmus Lema, 'China's Investments in Renewable Energy in Africa: Creating Co-benefits or Just Cashing-In?', *World Development* 141 (2021): 1–18.
14. Such as donations, interest-free loans, discount loans, technical assistance, project construction, direct factory construction, expert guidance, labour services, personnel training, technical training, technical management guidance, preferential loans, investment and trade, construction, heavily indebted poor countries' debt relief, training for trade officials, natural disaster emergency aid, etc.
15. Christopher Alessi and Beina Xu, 'China in Africa', Council on Foreign Affairs, 2015, https://www.cfr.org/china/china-africa/p9557.

and investment support.... It should of course also be noted that China is by no means alone in prioritising development relationships with countries of strategic or commercial significance to itself.'[16]

Third, the operational costs of Chinese companies, such as labour and equipment costs, are more competitive compared to many international majors.[17] Chinese labour is considered to be highly diligent, effective, and disciplined, but with lesser social demands compared to Western labour.[18] Furthermore, the lower costs of Chinese projects are especially attractive to many of these developing countries.

Challenges to Chinese investment in Africa

Although there is extensive room for Sino-African cooperation, there are still a number of obstacles at both domestic and regional levels.

International competition in Africa

China is not the only player in the African energy sector, and always have to either compete or work with other international players. For example, CNPC is a relative newcomer in the Mozambique LNG industry. After CNPC's investment, Eni, an Italian energy company, remains the indirect owner of 50%of the participation in gas block, Area 4. Other than these two major players, Empresa Nacional de Hidrocarbonetos from Mozambique, Kogas from Korea, and Galp Energia from Portugal evenly share the remaining 30 per cent of participants. Companies from Japan, Thailand, and Malaysia also operate in other gas blocks in the region. Therefore, China faces severe competition in Africa and cannot only rely on bilateral ties with African countries to support their energy investment.

Domestic conflicts

While domestic insecurity is a concern for many investors in Africa, Chinese energy companies tend to 'fill the space' in the African energy market, such as South Sudan, where Western powers are unwilling to or find it risky to invest. However, such an approach could expose Chinese investors to high security risks. For example, in South Sudan, clashes between rebel forces and the South Sudanese government have caused over 1,000 fatalities and have reduced oil

---

16. Hannah Edinger, 'Colonial Ambitions?' *New Matilda*, 2008, https://newmatilda.com/2008/08/11/colonial-ambitions.
17. Edward Friedman, 'China-Driven Development as China Pours Billions into Africa, Other Countries Are Trying to Keep Up', *Beijing Review*, 1 February 2009, http://www.bjreview.com/world/txt/2009-02/01/content_176304.htm.
18. Ibid.

flows by 20%.[19] Such conflicts have forced China to impose a rare overt political intervention in the region, calling for an immediate end to hostilities and the protection of vital oilfields from rebels.

Business cultural differences

There are a number of regional, ethnic, and cultural differences between China and Africa. Due to cultural differences, both parties fail to engage in smooth communication, and the progress in cooperation is therefore affected. Moreover, different business practices and losses in translation unavoidably increase the cost of cooperation.

Local grievance towards Chinese presence

The Chinese presence in Africa is not always idyllic. The movement of thousands of Chinese migrants into Africa has become a source of social issues in the continent. Although the Chinese investors have limited direct contact with the local population, grievances towards them have unavoidably been aggravated around social issues like unemployment. Growing resentment in African society has resulted in conflicts and violent incidents.

China's Energy Diplomacy in Africa

A historical review

The China-Africa energy relationship can be viewed within the broader picture of the China-Africa relationship, which began as a strategic partnership. Before the 1990s, China's diplomacy in Africa mainly focused on building political relations, but it extended to energy cooperation after China started importing oil from Africa in 1992. Due to increasing import dependency, stability in the overseas oil supply is of great significance to China's economic growth and social development. Diversification of overseas energy supply became a top strategic agenda, and the resource-rich Africa fit in perfectly here. China's energy diplomacy in Africa, with oil as a focus, can be divided into three stages: 1950–1979, 1980–1999, and 2000 onwards.

China's first Chairman Mao Zedong and former Premier Zhou Enlai's visits to Africa in the early 1960s are regarded as the start of the Sino-African diplomatic relationship because they won the friendship of many African nations and extended China's diplomatic reach to them.[20] China's the

---

19. David Smith, 'China Urges Immediate End to Conflict in South Sudan', *Guardian*, 6 January 2014.
20. Ting'en Lu, 'The Example of Summit Diplomacy between China and African Premier Zhou Enlai's First Visit to Africa', in *China and Africa*, ed. Center for African Studies, Peking

diplomatic relations with Africa laid a political foundation for future oil diplomacy, especially with resource-rich countries such as Sudan, Nigeria, Libya, Egypt, and others. The close political cooperation with these countries was a prelude to Sino-African energy diplomatic relations.

In the 1980s, China and African countries moved beyond political diplomacy and began to embark on economic cooperation. Leadership meetings and summits were channels for applying China's diplomatic principles and maintaining confidence in the Sino-African relationship. In the 1990s, China and a few oil-producing countries in Africa, such as Angola and Sudan, engaged in petroleum cooperation. At this point, oil diplomacy between China and Africa had three characteristics: first, there were no mature regulations and standards; second, the form of cooperation was monotonous and not abundant; and third, there were few countries in Africa that engaged in petroleum diplomacy with China. Nevertheless, China accumulated practical experience of independent investment in energy projects and increased its competitiveness in the international petroleum market.

In general, before the twenty-first century, China's energy shortage problems were not so serious, and its oil imports from Africa accounted for only one-fifth of its total oil imports. Therefore, both importing energy resources was not a top priority to China and the China-Africa energy cooperation policies were implemented loosely. However, it still cultivated a favourable environment for China's oil enterprises to enter the African market and enhance the energy cooperation in the following years.

In early 2000s, China dependency on foreign oil was driven by rapid economic development. To ensure supply security, China promoted the diversification of energy imports, boosting African oil and gas cooperation. Under the going-out strategy, Chinese NOCs took the initiative to expand their upstream asset portfolio in Africa. Both sides started to move beyond oil trade and collaborate in other energy fields, such as upstream development and renewable energy.

China also attempted to formalise the principles underpinning its energy diplomacy in Africa with a high-level policy framework. In 2006, in order to formalise long-term trade and investment with Africa, China issued China's African Policy.[21] China and African countries established the FOCAC, which is a multilateral platform for Chinese and African leaders to meet and promote Sino-African cooperation. Energy investment in Africa remains a key element in China's relationship with African countries and has been further incorporated into the BRI.

University (Beijing: Peking University Press, 2005).
21. PRC State Council, 'Government Issues African Policy Paper', PRC State Council, 2006, http://www.gov.cn/misc/2006-01/12/content_156509.htm.

High-level meetings as the key channels

Over the last three decades, Chinese leaders frequently visited Africa to build energy relationships. A key objective of China's oil diplomacy in Africa is to strengthen the diversification of energy supply sources in order to enhance energy security and reduce China's oil dependence on the Middle East.[22] Closer economic ties are also expected to enhance political trust between China and Africa.

In 1996, former Chinese President Jiang Zemin visited Egypt, Kenya, Ethiopia, Mali, Namibia, and Zimbabwe, pinning down a series of energy cooperation.[23] In 2004, former Premier Wen Jiabao visited the oil-producing Libya in 2003, and former President Hu Jintao visited other resource-rich countries, including Egypt, Gabon, and Algeria.[24] In 2006, leaders of forty-eight African countries gathered in the China-Africa Cooperation Forum in Beijing. They reached a consensus and made plans on energy cooperation.[25] To further consolidate this partnership with African countries, former President Hu Jintao visited five African countries in 2009 to promote China-Africa energy cooperation.[26] From 2009 to 2012, over seventy top leaders from China and Africa visited each other in high-level events,[27] followed by the signing of new energy agreements.

In 2000, the Chinese government officially relaxed requirements for overseas investment and encouraged companies to build factories in Africa. Chinese NOCs also stepped up their effort to promote development alongside their investment in Africa; for example, through the construction of various public facilities.[28] The Chinese government also decided to support selected Chinese banks to set up the China and Africa Development Fund, with an initial fund of US$500 million.[29] The bilateral trade and economic cooperation between China and Africa has grown rapidly, and cooperation has expanded in several fields relevant to policy, economy, science, education, culture, public

---

22. Ibid.
23. Xinhua News, 'Memorabilia of Chinese Presidents' Visits in Africa', *Xinhua News*, 24 March 2013, http://news.xinhuanet.com/world/2013-03/24/c_124496931.htm.
24. PRC MFA, 'China and African Countries Celebrate the 50th Anniversary of Diplomatic Relations', PRC MFA, 2006, http://www.fmprc.gov.cn/ce/cebw/eng/xnyfgk/t257854.htm.
25. Ibid.
26. PRC MFA, 'Hu Jintao's Speech: Work Together to Write a New Chapter of China-Africa Friendship', PRC MFA, 2009, http://www.fmprc.gov.cn/mfa_eng/wjdt_665385/zyjh_665391/t538257.shtml.
27. PRC MFA, 'Follow-Up of the Fourth FOCAC Ministerial Meeting', PRC MFA, 2012, https://www.mfa.gov.cn/ce/cerw//chn/rdzt/t952918.htm.
28. PRC MFA, 'Vice Minister of Commerce Wei Jianguo: China-Africa Economic and Trade Cooperation with Impressive Results', PRC MFA, 2006, http://www.gov.cn/zwhd/2006-01/13/content_157162.htm.
29. PRC State Council, 'China Trade Cooperation with Africa', PRC State Council, 2010, http://www.gov.cn/zwgk/2010-12/23/content_1771638.htm.

health, social affairs, and peace and security.[30] The scale and scope of these types of cooperation were expanded under China's African Policy (2006) and the BRI framework.

South-South cooperation

The Chinese government often emphasises that Chinese energy investment in Africa is part of the country's promotion of the 'South-South cooperation'. Apart from investments and discounted loans, China has helped African countries with the construction of public facilities, from roads to schools and hospitals. Under the South-South cooperation framework, Chinese companies assist African countries with development as part of their investment projects. For example, in 1995, China combined the aid provided to Sudan with an oil project in the country. In this project, while Sudan enjoyed preferential government loans from China at a discounted rate, Chinese NOC entered Sudan's upstream sector and participated in production.[31] Some scholars have argued that China's aid to Sudan, particularly that invested in its oil industry, is an important factor for why the African oil producer became the source of Africa's largest oil exports to China.[32] Although the increasing footprint of Chinese national companies in Africa still reportedly led to a number of social unrest incidents, from anti-Chinese sentiment to unemployment of local people,[33] these investments and aids were still well received by the African governments and in turn enhanced the energy cooperation between China and Africa.

Climate cooperation

Climate cooperation is another key focus in the broader energy relationships between China and Africa that drives multilateral cooperation. Although conventional infrastructure projects have predominantly characterised China's energy engagement with African countries over the last three decades, the signature of the Paris Agreement has gradually shifted their cooperation towards a more sustainability-centred one. The announcement of Chinese President Xi Jinping in 2021 to stop funding Chinese overseas coal-fired projects (including

---

30. FOCAC Archives. 2006. 'China Looking for Redoubled Cooperation with Africa', accessed 11 November 2015, http://www.focac.org/eng/zt/zgdfzzcwj/t231169.htm; http://www.focac.org/eng/zt/zgdfzzcwj/t231169.htm.
31. PRC MOFCOM, 'Country Guide for Foreign Investment and Cooperation: Sudan (2021)', PRC MOFCOM, 2021, http://www.mofcom.gov.cn/dl/gbdqzn/upload/sudan.pdf.
32. Chunrong Tian, 'Analysis on Import and Export of Chinese Petroleum in 2002', *International Petroleum Economics* 3 (2003): 6.
33. George Ofosu and David Sarpong, 'China in Africa: On the Competing Perspectives of the Value of Sino-Africa Business Relationships', *Journal of Economic Issues* 56, no. 1 (2022): 137–157.

those in Africa) was considered a milestone of the above shift, with energy companies and policy banks following suit. For example, China Development Bank signed a MOU with Green Climate Fund to facilitate multilateral cooperation in Africa. Power China was also actively exploring and contracting renewable energy projects in the region.

In the same year, China and 53 African countries signed a ground-breaking declaration—the Sino-African Declaration on Climate Change, presenting a long and exhaustive list of climate cooperation between China and Africa. The joint declaration reflected that structural changes are now on the energy cooperation between China and African countries.[34] Alongside South-South cooperation, a 'climate partner' has become China's new identity in relation to African countries. It also reflected that consideration of public goods around climate rather than merely commercial gains are added to their energy cooperation. Chinse investors started to increase their investment in projects with greater environmental co-benefits to the local community in Africa, such as climate change adaptation and energy poverty. Although these projects depart from traditional investment and financing models by SOEs and policy banks, they add extra momentum to green cooperation between China and Africa, especially in the area of technology cooperation.

China's Energy Cooperation via the FOCAC

In order to promote China's multilateral cooperation and dialogue with Africa, the policy identifies the FACOC as an effective mechanism and assigns importance to its follow-up action plans. The FOCAC, established in 2000, is a multilateral platform for dialogue and cooperation between China and African countries, covering various aspects of politics, economy, trade, society, and culture.[35] The FOCAC represented a new strategic partnership model between China and Africa in solving global issues, including those to do with energy. According to an official FOCAC document, the basis of the forum is 'political equality and mutual trust, economic win-win cooperation, and two-way cultural exchanges, opening a new chapter in China-Africa relationship'.[36] While some scholars have argued that China established the FOCAC for its grand strategy, African countries were keen to use the forum as a means to attract Chinese investment.[37]

---

34. Wei Shen, 'China-Africa Declaration on Climate Change: Old Wine in New Bottles?', IDS, 2021, https://www.ids.ac.uk/opinions/china-africa-declaration-on-climate-change-old-wine-in-new-bottles/.
35. FOCAC, 'To Achieve Common Development and Prosperity through Joint Efforts of China and Africa', FOCAC Achieves, 2012, http://www.focac.org/eng/ltda/t967201.htm.
36. Ibid.
37. Ana Cristina Alves, 'Chinese Economic Diplomacy in Africa: The Lusophone Strategy', in *China Returns to Africa: A Rising Power and a Content Embrace*, ed. Chris Alden, Daniel Large, and Ricardo Soares de Oliveira (Oxford University Press, 2008), 69–82; Mwesiga Baregu,

Energy cooperation is considered a key aspect of promoting the FOCAC. The FOCAC's Ministerial Conference 2000 was held in Beijing on 12 October, and the Programme for China-Africa Cooperation in Economic and Social Development was signed during the closing ceremony. The programme highlighted that China and Africa had realised the importance of natural resources.[38] China and Africa were set to establish strategic partnerships in multiple areas, including trade and resource production. The forum was used to help Africa improve its production capacity and realise export diversification.[39] This agenda aligned with China's broader strategy, from the going-out strategy to the BRI.

There have been seven FOCAC ministerial conferences to date. They are held every three years and alternate between China and an African country. Since the first FOCAC in Beijing, the Chinese government has paid great attention to the follow-up work of the event. The Chinese government established a follow-up action committee consisting of more than twenty ministries and commissions to guarantee the implementation of the commitment made at the forum. The first event identified the need to promote Chinese investment in African resource projects, especially those related to critical minerals that are the key to clean technology.[40]

The second conference in 2003 paid attention to the new measures that could be adopted to deepen cooperation on human resource development, agriculture, infrastructure, investment, and trade. The conference passed the FOCAC Addis Ababa Action Plan (2004–2006), which mapped out a three-year programme for China-Africa cooperation in political, economic, trade, and social development as well as other areas. The Chinese government pledged to open up the market and grant tariff-free market access to some commodities from the least developed countries in Africa.[41] Both sides agreed to strengthen their consultations on cooperation in natural resources exploration, particularly energy development, and work out the modalities to promote these objectives.[42]

This was the first ministerial conference ever held in Africa, and a matter of great significance in China-Africa relations. The conference highlighted the cooperation between Chinese and African companies. The first China-Africa Business Conference was held in parallel with the Second Ministerial

---

'The Three Faces of the Dragon: Tanzania-China Relations in Historical Perspective', in *Crouching Tiger, Hidden Dragon? Africa and China*, ed. Kweku Ampiah and Sanusha Naidu (Scottsville: University of KwaZulu-Natal Press, 2008), 197–219.

38. FOCAC, 'Programme for China-Africa Cooperation in Economic and Social Development', FOCAC Archives, 2009, http://www.focac.org/eng/ltda/dyjbzjhy/DOC12009/t606797.htm.
39. Ibid.
40. Ibid.
41. FOCAC, 'Forum on China-Africa Cooperation: Addis Ababa Action Plan', FOCAC Archives, 2004, http://www.focac.org/eng/ltda/dejbzjhy/DOC22009/.
42. Ibid.

Conference with over 500 Chinese and African entrepreneurs attending. Twenty-one agreements were signed with a total value of US$1 billion.[43]

The year 2006 was the fiftieth year since China had started diplomatic relations with African countries. It also marked China's consolidation of its Africa policy that put Sino-African cooperation forward in a more multilateral way. Both parties have attempted to look for 'redoubled cooperation' to deal with international or regional affairs, having adopted a policy document to strengthen their ties. China's Africa Policy in 2006 highlighted that 'China is ready to enhance consultation and coordination with Africa within multilateral trade systems and financial institutions and work together to urge the UN and other international organisations to pay more attention to the question of economic development, promote South-South cooperation, push forward the establishment of a just and rational multilateral trade system, and make the voices of developing countries heard in the decision-making of international financial affairs. It will step up cooperation with other countries and international organisations to support the development of Africa and help realise Millennium Development Goals in Africa.'[44]

In the same year, the Third Ministerial Conference was held with forty-eight African countries and twenty-four representatives from international and regional organisations.[45] The conference passed the Declaration of the Beijing Summit of the Forum on China-Africa Cooperation and the FOCAC Beijing Action Plan (2007–2009). Both sides also agreed to 'promote joint exploration and rational exploitation of energy and other resources through diversified forms of cooperation', let China 'help African countries turn their advantages in energy and resources into development strengths', and 'step up scientific and technological cooperation in areas of common interest including solar energy and mining'.[46] Moreover, four key decisions influencing China-Africa energy cooperation were made in the conference. China decided to double its 2006 assistance to Africa by 2009, providing preferential loans of US$3 billion, preferential buyer's credits of US$2 billion and a development fund of US$5 billion to the continent.[47]

The second China-Africa Business Conference was held in parallel with the Third Ministerial Conference. Former Chinese Premier Wen Jiabao had five suggestions on strengthening China-Africa cooperation: to expand the size of China-Africa trade; to increase cooperation in investment; to upgrade assistance to Africa; to promote cooperation between the business communities;

---

43. PRC MFA, 'FOCAC Ministerial Meetings and Beijing Summits', PRC MFA, 2012, https://www.mfa.gov.cn/ce/cemg//chn/zt/zfhzlt/t982253.htm.
44. PRC MFA, 'Chinese Government Issues African Policy Paper', PRC MFA, https://www.mfa.gov.cn/ce/cegh//eng/xwdt/t231007.htm.
45. Ibid.
46. FOCAC, 'Forum on China-Africa Cooperation Beijing Action Plan (2007–2009)', FOCAC Archives, http://www.focac.org/eng/ltda/dscbzjhy/DOC32009/t280369.htm.
47. Ibid.

and to increase assistance to Africa in human resources development. Together with China's Africa Policy, this year's Summit demonstrated the Chinese government's devotion to developing its strategic partnership with Africa more pragmatically, allowing the business communities to advance their economic and energy cooperation.

The Fourth Ministerial Conference of the FOCAC in Sharm el-Sheikh passed the Declaration of Sharm el-Sheikh of the FOCAC and the FOCAC Sharm el-Sheikh Action Plan (2010–2012). The documents proposed eight new measures to strengthen China-Africa cooperation, and at least four of them were related to energy. First, it included the establishment of a China-Africa partnership in addressing climate change by consulting with senior officials from time to time, thereby enhancing cooperation on satellite weather monitoring, development and utilisation of new energy sources, prevention and control of desertification, and urban environmental protection. China decided to build 100 clean-energy projects for Africa covering solar power, bio-gas, and small hydropower.[48] The second of these measures was to enhance cooperation with Africa in science and technology. China proposed to launch a China-Africa science and technology partnership, which covered the energy field. China would carry out 100 joint demonstration projects on scientific and technological research, receive 100 African postdoctoral fellows to conduct scientific research in China, and assist these fellows in going back and serving their home countries.[49] The two other measures were to help Africa develop its financing capacity, covering the area of energy, and to open up China's market to African products.[50]

The Fifth Ministerial Conference of the FOCAC was held in 2012, again in Beijing, and passed the Beijing Declaration of the Fifth Ministerial Conference of the Forum on China-Africa Cooperation and the Beijing Action Plan (2013–2015). The document presented more proposals on energy cooperation, which included prioritising energy infrastructure, supporting joint development and the proper use of Africa's energy and resources through enterprises, helping African countries translate their energy and resource strengths into development strength, and advancing cooperation in clean energy and renewable resources projects in keeping with the principles of mutual benefit and sustainable development.[51]

The Sixth FOCAC was held in Johannesburg in 2015. As part of the BRI, China offered large funding packages to boost cooperation in a broad range

---

48. PRC MFA, 'FOCAC Ministerial Meetings and Beijing Summits', PRC MFA, 2012, https://www.mfa.gov.cn/ce/cemg//chn/zt/zfhzlt/t982253.htm; FOCAC, Forum on China-Africa Cooperation Sharm El Sheikh Action Plan (2010–2012)', FOCAC Archives, 2009, http://www.focac.org/eng/ltda/dsjbzjhy/hywj/t626387.htm.
49. Ibid.
50. Ibid.
51. FOCAC, 'The Fifth Ministerial Conference of the Forum on China-Africa Cooperation Beijing Action Plan (2013–2015)', FOCAC Archives, 2012, http://www.focac.org/eng/ltda/dwjbzjjhys/hywj/t954620.htm.

of areas, such as agriculture, energy, green development, and infrastructure. China pledged to 'offer USD 60 billion of funding support, including USD 5 billion of free aid and interest-free loans, USD 35 billion of preferential loans and export credit on more favourable terms, USD 5 billion of additional capital for the China-Africa Development Fund and the Special Loan for the Development of African SMEs each, and a China-Africa production capacity cooperation fund with the initial capital of 10 billion dollars'.[52]

The seventh FOCAC took place in Beijing in 2018. An action plan was adopted to call for the further development of China-Africa cooperation. In particular, the BRI has played a significant role in Chinese investment in Africa. More African leaders attended the FOCAC in 2018 than the UN General Assembly meeting, which was held around the same time. These disparities in attendance reflected the shifting dynamics and priorities of African countries.[53]

The eighth FOCAC took place in Dakar in 2021 and announced a joint declaration on climate change.[54] China and fifty-three African countries announced their visions to strengthen cooperation in areas such as climate change, green energy, and low-carbon infrastructure projects. The declaration was expected to have profound implications for China's energy cooperation with African countries.[55]

The following two FOCACs were incorporated into the BRI, which serves as a roadmap for China's international engagement. It is estimated that sub-Saharan Africa will receive up to 25% of BRI investments in the 2020s.[56] China also reaffirmed clean energy as a key aspect in its energy cooperation with Africa, by promoting joint projects on solar power, bio-gas, and small hydropower. In the joint clean energy projects, China cooperates with eleven African countries on new energy programmes to help them deal with the multiple effects of climate change. As a developing region, Africa requires funding and technology. China's aid in new energy functions as a package covering technology, funding, management, knowledge, etc. The FOCAC and its follow-up actions have strengthened energy cooperation between China and Africa by facilitating diplomatic engagement, trade, investment, security cooperation, and cultural exchange between China and African countries.

---

52. Xinhua News, 'Xi Announces 10 Major Programs to Boost China-Africa Cooperation in Coming 3 Years', *Xinhua News*, 4 December 2015.
53. Abdi Latif Dahir, 'Twice as Many African Presidents Made It to China's Africa Summit Than to the UN General Assembly', *Quartz Africa*, 5 October 2018.
54. PRC MEE, 'China-Africa Declaration on Climate Change', PRC MEE, 2021, https://www.mee.gov.cn/ywdt/hjywnews/202112/t20211202_962652.shtml.
55. Wei Shen, 'China-Africa Declaration on Climate Change: Old Wine in New Bottles?', IDS, 2021, https://www.ids.ac.uk/opinions/china-africa-declaration-on-climate-change-old-wine-in-new-bottles/.
56. Bee Chun Boo, 'China Aims for Win-Win Partnership with African Mining Sector', *Baker McKenzie*, 2020, https://www.bakermckenzie.com/en/insight/publications/2020/01/china-partnership-with-african-mining-sector.

Multilateralism in China-Africa Energy Cooperation

Expanding volume and scope of energy cooperation with African requires a broader facilitation platform beyond bilateral agreements. China's Africa Policy claims that it 'is ready to enhance consultation and coordination with Africa within multilateral trade systems and financial institutions' and 'will hold regular/irregular consular consultations with African countries . . . in bilateral or multilateral consular relations in order to improve understanding and expand cooperation'.[57] These claims laid down the multilateral foundation for both sides to 'encourage and support competent Chinese enterprises to cooperate with African nations' especially in the area.[58]

Climate change has given China extra momentum to multilateral cooperation with African countries, given their consensus to promote energy transition collectively. African countries naturally sit in China's implementation of the Belt and Road South-South Cooperation Initiative on Climate Change. They also fit well in China's pledges to make its overseas projects more environmentally sustainable and expand the export of new energy technology and products. The latest documents, such as the China-Africa Declaration on Climate Change, are expected to have some profound implications for China's energy and climate cooperation with Africa.

Multilateral platform such as the FOCAC was also considered to be a more feasible platform for China to advance its South-South cooperation. Hosting the FOCAC in Beijing every six years is key to increasing China's involvement and gaining consensus. In the longer-term, the FOCAC has become the lynchpin of Sino-African relations. Driven by a joint ministerial conference held every three years since 2000, the FOCAC emphasises the planned cultivation of a long-term relationship based on solidarity and cooperation. This platform has strengthened Sino-African cooperation in all spheres. Through the FOCAC, China has facilitated market access, promoted energy cooperation, enhanced climate cooperation, promoted duty-free treatment, improved trade structure, and eased Africa's debt. China also intends to settle trade disputes via bilateral and multilateral approaches in the FOCAC. In short, the FOCAC has provided China with a standard platform to strengthen its economic and energy interests.

The implementation of multilateral cooperation via the FOCAC, however, was not always effective, and there are three underlying factors. First, while Beijing appears to have a high-level strategic concept for its engagement with Africa, the actual implementation has not been a monotonous exercise. Some studies have even questioned whether the actions of the energy firms have always aligned with China's foreign policy goals. James Swan noted in a June 2008 Congressional testimony that 'there are often exaggerated charges

---

57. PRC MFA, 'Chinese Government Issues African Policy Paper', PRC MFA, https://www.mfa.gov.cn/ce/cegh//eng/xwdt/t231007.htm.
58. Ibid.

that Chinese firms' activities or investment decisions are coordinated by the Chinese government as some sort of strategic gambit in the high-stakes game of global energy security. In reality, Chinese firms compete for profitable projects not only with more technologically and politically savvy international firms, but also with each other.'[59] Moreover, poor investment performance, especially in risk regions such as Sudan, reflected that Chinese NOCs were still in their learning stage, gaining experience from their global expansion.[60]

Second, while China's Africa Policy was a systematic outline of China's policy for Africa, it lacked concrete follow-up plans for energy cooperation between the two sides. Most of these documents introduced a long list of relevant fields for cooperation, but did not always elaborate on the precise methods, scale of cooperation, or responsible stakeholders. Similarly, the policies originating from the FOCAC are often too broad to be implemented. Without a well-organised governance structure, the influence of the FOCAC is limited.

Third, the FOCAC lacks the legal mechanism to ensure China's energy investment and energy security in Africa, which thus have to rely on government-to-government agreements. For example, since 2005, China has granted tariff-free treatment to over thirty of the least developed African countries for 190 types of commodities. These mutually beneficial agreements and policies undoubtedly have contributed to China-Africa trade relations, but most of these agreements are considered as governmental guidance instead of a broader multilateral legal framework. Therefore, China has tended to rely on traditional government agreements for managing its trade relations with African countries.

With the weakening influence of Western countries in Africa, China's experience in promoting South-South cooperation allowed it to gain a better ideological advantage in Africa to propose energy investment, set policy agendas, and formulate new system rules.[61] Nevertheless, ever since China and African countries proposed multilateral cooperation in 2006, they have not always agreed with the actual plan for this cooperation. Therefore, although the FOCAC provides China with another promising multilateral channel to develop its energy diplomacy with Africa, actual implementation appears to be limited.

---

59. James Swan, 'China in Africa: Implications for U.S. Policy', US Senate Committee on Foreign Relations, 2008, http://www.foreign.senate.gov/imo/media/doc/Christensen Testimony080604a.pdf.
60. A Beijing-based think tank, interview with the author, 2013.
61. Ana Cristina Alves, 'Chinese Economic Diplomacy in Africa: The Lusophone Strategy', in *China Enters Africa: A Rising Power and a Content Embrace*, ed. Chris Alden, Daniel Large, and Ricardo Soares de Oliveira (London: Hurst, 2008); Mwesiga Baregu, 'The Three Faces of the Dragon: Tanzania-China Relations in Historical Perspective', in *Crouching Tiger, Hidden Dragon? Africa and China*, ed. Kweku Ampiah and Sanusha Naidu (Scottsville: University of KwaZulu-Natal Press, 2008), 197–219.

5
China-EU Energy Cooperation

A Partnership in Low-Carbon Transition

Historically, China and the EU did not consider each other as major energy trade partners, but China signing the Paris Agreement has further driven potential clean energy cooperation between China and the EU. Both powers are committed to a comprehensive strategic partnership—EU-China 2020 Strategic Agenda for Cooperation, where climate change is a key policy agenda.[1] As a leader in low-carbon transition, the EU sees China as part of the solution to climate change. As such, China needs a partner that has mastered such technologies and, more importantly, is open to technology cooperation.[2] This creates common interests in cooperation in the area of energy technologies, such as energy efficiency and renewable energy sources.

Over the last three decades, China and the EU issued a series of supporting policies to promote clean energy development, which established a foundation for clean technology cooperation. In 2005, China published the Renewable Energy Law of the People's Republic of China. The law establishes the basic legal system and policy framework for developing renewable energy.[3] China's 12th Five-Year Plan on the development of renewable energy marked a new page for renewables development in China, emphasizing quality over quantity. China planned to create a competitive clean energy industry system, including wind power, solar power, nuclear power, and other non-fossil energies. Additionally, the plan stated that China would continue its

---

1. European Commission, 'EU-China 2020 Strategic Agenda for Cooperation', European Commission, 2013, https://www.eeas.europa.eu/sites/default/files/20131123.pdf.
2. Giovanni Grevi and Vasconcelos Alvaro, 'Partnerships for Effective Multilateralism: EU Relations with Brazil, China, India and Russia', *Chaillot Paper* 109 (2008), http://www.iss.europa.eu/publications/detail/article/partnerships-for-effective-multilateralism-eu-relations-with-brazil-china-india-and-russia/.
3. PRC NPC, 'Renewable Energy Law of the People's Republic of China', PRC NPC, 2005, http://www.npc.gov.cn/zgrdw/englishnpc/Law/2007-12/13/content_1384096.htm.

international cooperation efforts in the field of clean energy to break the development bottleneck in technology.[4]

Along with the same agenda, China's energy white papers in 2012 and 2020 repeatedly asserted China's ambition to increase its reliance on renewable energy as a long-term option for decarbonising its economy.[5] In October 2021, China released a new decarbonisation framework—Action Plan for Carbon Dioxide Peaking Before 2030, restating the country's goal for 2025 and 2030.[6] By 2030, it aims to lower the share of fossil fuels in China's energy consumption to 75%, while also targeting a 65% drop in carbon emissions per unit of GDP from its 2005 level. Furthermore, it sets out to curb the development of projects with high energy consumption and emissions.

Regarding promoting clean energy, the EU has provided leadership and support at a very early stage. It published a series of policy documents and established a support plan and evaluation mechanism to implement its clean energy policy.[7] These policy initiatives have become the foundation for China and the EU to enhance collaboration in areas of mutual interest related to the management of the energy system—on both the supply and demand sides—as well as other relevant cross-cutting issues.

The Foundation of China-EU Energy Cooperation

Energy cooperation between China and the EU, particularly in clean energy, has a long history and is mainly carried out in two categories: (1) personnel exchange and training, and (2) technology transfer and joint research and development.

Personnel exchange and training

Personnel exchange and training are long-term means of cooperation in the EU-China clean energy sector. Personnel exchanges between the two sides can

---

4. PRC State Council, 'An Overview of China Renewable Energy Twelfth Five Year Plan', PRC State Council, 2013, http://www.gov.cn/zwgk/2013-01/23/content_2318554.htm.
5. PRC State Council, *China's Energy Policy 2012* (Beijing: PRC State Council Information Office, 2012); PRC State Council, *Energy in China's New Era* (Beijing: PRC State Council Information Office, 2020).
6. PRC NDRC, 'Action Plan for Carbon Dioxide China', PRC NDRC, 2021, https://en.ndrc.gov.cn/policies/202110/t20211027_1301020.html.
7. For example, European Commission, 'A 2030 Framework for Climate and Energy Policies', European Commission, 2021, https://ec.europa.eu/clima/eu-action/climate-strategies-targets/2030-climate-energy-framework_en; European Commission, 'A European Strategy for Sustainable, Competitive and Secure Energy', European Commission, 2006, https://eur-lex.europa.eu/EN/legal-content/summary/green-paper-a-european-strategy-for-sustainable-competitive-and-secure-energy.html; European Commission, 'Communication from the Commission—Energy for the Future: Renewable Sources of Energy—White Paper for a Community Strategy and Action Plan', European Commission, 1997.

be roughly divided into high-level government exchanges, energy management personnel exchanges, and technical personnel exchanges. Due to the advanced capabilities of the EU in energy management, energy-saving, and environmental protection technology, the European talent shared with China to provide training on these three aspects has always been the main form of personnel exchanges between China and Europe.[8]

An early example is the China-EU Energy Training Programme. It cultivated a large number of energy professionals for China, which was understood to have helped improve energy efficiency, protect the environment, and promote sustainable development in the country. The EU energy experts advocated clean technology and promoted technology transfer in this programme.[9] These training programmes were organised more frequently in recent years due to increasing policy emphasis on energy-saving, environmental protection, and clean technology. During the training sessions, the two sides carried out discussions and consultations on common challenges and existing problems, and also share successful experiences.[10] As such, bilateral EU personnel exchanges were enhanced and were beneficial to popularise, utilise, and marketise clean energy technologies.

Technology transfer and joint R&D

EU-China energy cooperation has a strong focus on technology transfer. In the early 2000s, China claimed to treat the development of energy, water resources, and environmental protection technology as the priority of international technology cooperation, thus strengthening its interaction with the EU in clean energy technology as well as international cooperation projects for clean development mechanisms.[11] To gain access to the Chinese market, European energy companies often transfer their technologies to their Chinese partners. While, in recent years, China has become a world leader in manufacturing clean energy technology, from wind turbines and solar cells to lithium batteries for vehicles, international cooperation still plays an important role to Chinas R&D of clean energy innovation.

Both sides have increased their information sharing and experience exchange in clean energy innovation by setting up joint R&D for China and EU enterprises. For example, the China and EU Clean Energy Centre (EC2), which started in April 2010 in Beijing, is a landmark project representing China and the EU's strengthened R&D cooperation. These instruments have allowed China to cooperate with EU Member States via platforms and projects

---

8. A former officer at a China-Europe joint clean energy center, interview with the author, 2013.
9. Ibid.
10. Ibid.
11. PRC MOST, '国际科技合作实施纲要' [Outline for Implementation of International Science and Technology Cooperation], PRC MOST, 2006.

established under the EU. They have also advanced the establishment of multiple functional and strategic mechanisms for long-term cooperation in terms of energy exchange.

China's Energy Relations with the EU and Its Member States

The EU-China energy relationship can be viewed through the broader lens of the EU-China relationship, which was a trading partnership. The development of the EU-China relationship has undergone three phases: (1) exploration and construction of the partnership, (2) deepening and maturing of bilateral ties, and (3) managing the relationship, particularly in the context of cooperation and competition.[12] Notably, while the EU is an international organisation with the highest level of integration in the world, each one of its 28 members, and even different regions of each state, differ in their degree of interest in the EU-China energy relationship. The states have formulated clean energy policies or developed plans that are unique to each other. Therefore, China is facing a group of diversified stakeholders when cooperating in the clean energy field. Its partners can be the EU as a whole, the central government or local governments of each Member State, or companies and academic institutions whose headquarters are situated in Member States.

A historical review

In the 1970s

China's energy cooperation with certain EU Member States only began after the reform and opening up of China in the 1970s.[13] After the establishment of a formal diplomatic relationship between China and the European Economic Community (EEC),[14] the two parties expanded their trade cooperation covering industry, agriculture, energy, environment, transportation, science, and development aid. Trade has remained a key means for the interaction of the two powers, as has the exchange of energy-related technology over the three phases.

Since the opening-up of China, trade has become a driving force in the EU-China partnership.[15] The fast-growing Chinese market has become an important target in the EU's policy agenda in Asia. Yet, neither China nor

---

12. Francis Snyder, *The European Union and China, 1949–2008: Basic Documents and Commentary* (Oxford: Hart Publishing, 2009).
13. This is discussed, in part, in Daojiong Zha and Weixing Hu, 'Promoting Energy Partnership in Beijing and Washington', *Washington Quarterly* 30, no. 4 (2007): 105–115.
14. EEC was an international organisation created by the Treaty of Rome of 1957. It was made to constitute the first of the three pillars of the EU and is today part of the EU.
15. Pietro De Matteis, 'EU-China Cooperation in the Field of Energy, Environment and Climate Change', *Journal of Contemporary European Research* 6, no. 4 (2010): 449–477.

the EU Member States considered energy as a key factor in their cooperation in the early 1970s. In 1978, China and the EU signed their first key accord—the Agreement between the People's Republic of China and the European Community—which established a new initiative to regulate trade-related issues between them.[16] This agreement also underpinned the ideology behind EU-China relations and remained at the heart of the bilateral partnership between the two powers.

In the 1980s and 1990s

The earliest cooperation between the two parties, the China-EU Energy Training Programme, was launched a year after a delegation from the European Commission Directorate-General for Energy (EC DG ENER) visited China. At the same time, China also began to involve certain EU Member States in its offshore oil development.[17] In 1985, the two powers signed the Agreement on Trade and Economic Cooperation, which was a new reference point for their relationship.

In the early 1990s, the EU began to see China as a rising power and 'an unprecedented series of summits between China and some of its key world partners had demonstrated China's wish to be recognised as a world power'.[18] A full-scale relationship between the two parties materialised in 1995, when the EU announced its first China policy paper; it stated, 'Europe must develop a long-term relationship with China that reflects China's worldwide, as well as regional, economic, and political influence. Europe's relations with China are bound to be a cornerstone of Europe's external relations, both with Asia and globally.'[19]

In the 2000s

Due to the increasing interdependency in economies, the EU and China became each other's major trading partners in the 2000s. While China has been the EU's largest source of imported goods since 2015, it has also become one of the

---

16. European Commission, 'The Agreement between the People's Republic of China and the European Community', European Commission, 1978, http://aei.pitt.edu/8243/1/31735055282234_1.pdf.
17. This is discussed, in part, in Zha Daojiong and H. Weixing, 'Promoting Energy Partnership in Beijing and Washington', *Washington Quarterly* 30, no. 4 (2007): 105–115.
18. European Commission, 'Building a Comprehensive Partnership with China', European Commission, 1998, https://eur-lex.europa.eu/LexUriServ/LexUriServ.do?uri=COM:1998:0181:FIN:EN:PDF.
19. European Commission, 'A Long-Term Policy for China-Europe Relations', European Commission, 1995, https://op.europa.eu/en/publication-detail/-/publication/0bcbc1c7-2c78-4bba-a027-f67035eeac4f.

EU's major export markets.[20] China and the EU have also carried out policy coordination through EU-China summits, the highest level of political meeting between the two, which started in 1998. To date, there have been seventeen of these summits. These meetings play a significant role in developing and deepening the relationship between China and the EU. During each summit, the two sides hold consultations on issues of common concern, and discuss issues related to politics, economics, etc. Since 2001, energy, especially clean energy, has become a key focus in these discussions, which is also reflected in the agreements signed during the summits and the joint statements issued after each summit.

The strategic partnership between China and the EU established in 2003 has enhanced China-EU energy cooperation, which was not a prominent focus in the earlier China-EU relationship. While China and the EU have undergone a dramatic transformation in recent decades, their common interests in energy cooperation and environmental issues have expanded because neither China nor any of the EU countries can solve these issues alone.[21] The two giants account for approximately one-third of the world's energy use, and their energy needs are expected to increase continuously to fuel their growing economies and populations. Energy has gradually become more prominent in interactions between China and its EU counterparts. In the face of climate change, the issues of high global energy consumption, volatility of international oil prices, and environmental degradation have brought the two powers closer together.[22]

2010s onwards

During this period, the Sino-EU energy cooperation was not limited to the traditional security of resources and price, extending to broader energy issues, including energy governance, climate change, improvement of energy efficiency, and conservation and research innovations. In the 16th EU Summit in 2013, A new EU-China Joint Declaration on Energy Security was signed, assuring 'open' access to each other's markets.[23] In addition to affirming the EU's agenda to develop beneficial energy partnerships with key third-world countries, the new agreement also set out China's new concept of energy security that called for 'mutually beneficial cooperation, diversified forms of development, and common energy security through coordination'.[24] In

---

20. European Commission, 'European Union, Trade with China', European Commission, 2021 https://webgate.ec.europa.eu/isdb_results/factsheets/country/details_china_en.pdf.
21. X. Zhang. '中欧能源合作的未来——基于能源安全与气候变化的分析' [Future of Sino-EU cooperation: Analysis base on energy security and climate change], *International Economic Cooperation* 3 (2012): 11–16.
22. Ibid.
23. Chao Zhang, 'The EU-China Energy Cooperation' (Briefing Paper, EIAS, 2017).
24. Ibid.

2016, China and the EU further laid out a roadmap to streamline their energy cooperation, with a focus on the transformation of their sustainable energy system.[25] Moreover, green energy and climate cooperation with the EU was also considered a key aspect in China's BRI.[26] These policy initiatives reflected a growing China-EU consensus about importance of climate change and sustainable development, paving the way for clean technology cooperation.

Energy Cooperation Mechanism between China and the EU

As the energy initiative progresses with official promotion, China and the EU have preliminarily established a structured cooperation mechanism, involving official channels and joint energy projects.

Official channels in China-EU clean energy cooperation

The China-EU Energy Conference, the China-Europe High-Level Energy Working Group, the China-Europe Energy Dialogue, and the EU-China Summit are the main official channels that facilitate China-Europe clean energy cooperation.

China-EU Energy Conference

In 1994, energy was first addressed as an individual agent in the China-EU Energy Conference, convened under the co-sponsorship of China's Ministry of Science and Technology (formerly the State Science and Technology Commission) and the EC DG ENER.[27] The conference is the largest-scale and highest-standard (ministerial level) energy event between China and the EU, offering a platform for Chinese and European ministries, enterprises, and experts to meet and share ideas.[28] To date, eight conferences have been held as China and the EU rotate to host the conference biennially. Every conference can invariably expect the attendance of a significant number of high-level industrial and government representatives. Topics on energy challenges commonly faced by both sides are discussed at the conference, which is not

---

25. European Commission, 'EU-China Roadmap on Energy Cooperation (2016–2020)', European Commission, 2016, https://ec.europa.eu/energy/sites/ener/files/documents/FINAL_EU_CHINA_ENERGY_ROADMAP_EN.pdf.
26. PRC NEA, 'Wang Yi on the Four Aspects of Developing China-Europe Union (EU) Relations', PRC NEA, 2020, https://obor.nea.gov.cn/detail2/14023.html; PRC NEA, 'More Opportunities for Green Cooperation as China, Europe Lead Fight against Climate Change', PRC NEA, 2020.
27. Ibid.
28. PRC MOST, '第八次中欧能源合作大会在上海召开' [The Eighth EU-China Energy Cooperation Conference held in Shanghai], PRC MOST, 2010, http://losangeles.china-consulate.org/chn/jbwzlm/ywzn/tech/news/201007/t20100727_5420927.htm.

only an official channel through which energy issues are communicated, but also a regular platform for Chinese and European energy corporations.

China-Europe High-Level Energy Working Group

The second China-EU Energy Conference in 1996 proposed the initiative of a bilateral energy working group.[29] A year later, a China-EU High-Level Energy Working Group was created to institutionalise the China-EU energy cooperation and provide guidance and supervision with a top-down approach.[30] The working group became a major platform for communications and collaboration among government officials and experts from both sides.

China-Europe Energy Dialogue

As the China-EU energy cooperation gained momentum, in 2005, China's NDRC and the EC DG Transport and Energy signed the Energy Dialogue Memorandum of Understanding with the objective to better coordinate each party's stance on energy issues and further cooperation. The dialogue is a deputy-ministerial-level meeting covering six prioritised areas, including renewable energy, energy efficiency, clean coal, nuclear energy, smart grid development, and energy law.[31]

As of 2013, a total of six Energy Dialogues[32] have been held between China and the EU. The first and second ones were held in 2007 and 2008, respectively, in the form of the Strategic Dialogue on Energy and Transport Strategies, and the others were held in the form of the EU-China Energy Dialogue. Both parties are known to exchange views and have reached a consensus on multiple energy issues. New steps have been taken towards practical cooperation. For instance, in the fifth China-EU Energy Dialogue, the NEA of China and the EC agreed to inaugurate a high-level energy conference held in Brussels in 2012, with the aim to set out directions and key areas of future practical cooperation. In 2013, the sixth EU-China Energy Dialogue covered issues such as energy strategy, energy market reform, low-carbon energy technologies, energy innovation regulation, and sustainable use of energy.[33] More importantly, a number of joint energy cooperative initiatives, such as

---

29. Chao Zhang, 'The EU-China Energy Cooperation' (Briefing Paper, EIAS, 2017).
30. European Commission, 'EU-China Energy Working Group Approved', European Commission, 1996, http://europa.eu/rapid/press-release_IP-96-1242_en.htm.
31. European Commission, 'Energy from Abroad', European Commission, 2014, http://ec.europa.eu/energy/international/bilateral_cooperation/china/china_en.htm.
32. The first and second were held in 2007 and 2008 respectively in the form of Strategic Dialogue on Energy and Transport Strategies. The others are in the form of EU-China Energy Dialogues.
33. PRC NEA, '第六次中欧能源对话在京举行' [The Sixth China-EU Energy Dialogue was held in Beijing]', PRC NEA, 2013, http://www.nea.gov.cn/2013-11/27/c_132923326.htm.

the Europe-China Clean Energy Centre (EC2), were formulated in the Energy Dialogue. These will be discussed in the next section.

EU-China Summit

For over a decade, China and the EU have held consultations on issues of common concerns such as politics and economy through the EU-China Summit. In these summits, Chinese and European leaders generally reach a relatively macro-level agreement on energy issues, especially on clean energy, and other energy cooperative mechanisms, such as the China-EU Energy Conference, the China and EU Energy Dialogue, and the China-EU High-Level Working Group. These summits also provide specialised platforms for both sides to further exchange information, coordinate specific clean energy policies, and act on the consensus. Through the leaders' Summit and Energy Dialogues, the two sides further consult on issues of global warming, environmental problems, the future development of clean energy, etc., and they engage in necessary policy coordination and reach various agreements on mutually beneficial premises.

A number of cooperative agreements have been signed, for example, the Euratom-China Research and Development Agreement at the 7th Summit in 2004, the Memorandum of Understanding on China-EU Dialogue on Energy and Transport Strategies at the 8th Summit in 2005, the Joint Statement on Europe-China Clean Energy Centre (EC2) at the 11th Summit in May 2009, and the Memorandum of Understanding on Cooperation Framework on Energy Performance and Quality in the Construction Sector at the 12th Summit in November 2009. These efforts not only laid the policy foundation for the China-EU cooperation in the clean energy sector, but also strongly promoted bilateral pragmatic cooperation in the sector—the specific cooperation agreements signed during the summits can best show this.

Energy programmes in China-EU clean energy cooperation

The above official channels have promoted the China-EU energy cooperation over the past three decades. Among a broad range of aspects covered, China and the EU have located their priorities in the promotion of clean energy, as reflected by the following energy programmes.

China-EU Energy Training Programme (from 1982 onwards)

The China-EU Energy Training Programme, established in 1982, is considered the earliest concrete project in the China-EU energy cooperation. This programme is organised every year to provide training courses for the Chinese. It symbolises the official start of the China-EU energy-management training project.³⁴ Since then, China-EU energy training centres have been gradually set up by Zhejiang Energy Research Institute, Tianjin Energy-Saving Technology Centre, Shanghai Energy Research Institute, and the Chongqing Energy-Saving Technology Service Centre.

Since 1982, every year, the five training centres have held one or two regular energy training classes, which are mainly taught by EU experts and professors and cover topics related to EU energy management and energy-saving technology.³⁵ In the beginning, European trainers were sent to China to conduct the training courses. In return, since 1995, Chinese trainees have been sent to Europe for training. Over 5,000 Chinese energy personnel are trained under this programme.³⁶ These training courses are expected to allow Chinese energy management staff from energy companies, government departments, and energy research institutions to grasp the latest developments of energy technology R&D in the EU.

Joint Energy and Environment Programme (from 2004 to the end of 2009)

In 2003, the NDRC and EC established the Joint Energy and Environment Programme (EEP) to push energy cooperation on both sides. As a five-year project, the EEP had four components, including energy policy development, energy efficiency, natural gas, and renewable energy. Cooperation in the clean energy sector plays an important role here, and its objectives include the utilisation of renewable energy by developing biomass resources in rural areas, producing power for villages in Western China, and developing policies concerning the use of offshore wind energy.³⁷ It had an investment of €42 million devoted to policy research, training programmes, personnel exchange, and technology transfer.³⁸

The programme was implemented in two phases: the first phase comprised ten large bidding projects involving offshore wind energy, biomass, and other sectors; the second phase provided EU grants for feasibility studies and demonstration projects in certain key areas in China. In the latter phase, projects related to clean energy were sub-projects of energy policy, energy efficiency, and renewable energy. At the end of 2009, the EEP was announced to cease with the basic completion of the projects over the two phases.³⁹ There

---

34. Chao Zhang, 'The EU-China Energy Cooperation' (Briefing Paper, EIAS, 2017); PRC MFA, 'China-EU Scientific and Technological Cooperation and Exchange', PRC MFA, 2004, http://www.fmprc.gov.cn/ce/cebe/eng/kj/t72211.htm.
35. Ibid.
36. Ibid.
37. Frank Haugwitz, 'EU-China Energy and Environment Program' (Presentation Paper, Conference of Wind Power Shanghai, 2007), http://www.frankhaugwitz.info/doks/aboutme/2007_11_02_EEP_RE_Shanghai_Wir_Power_Conference.pdf.
38. Ibid.
39. Ibid.

were a large number of practical results, such as demonstrating the feasibilities of offshore wind power and energy saving in key energy-consuming industries; more importantly, the projects were a strong and effective demonstration and actively promoted China in improving energy policy, energy efficiency, and the utilisation of renewable resources.

Europe-China Clean Energy Centre (EC2) (from 2010 to 2014)

In 2010, the NEA, MOC, and EC, with support from the Italian Ministry of Environment, Territory and Marine, launched the Europe-China Clean Energy Centre (EC2) at Tsinghua University to help the Chinese government promote clean energy use in China and create a more sustainable and efficient energy system.[40] In particular, this five-year cooperation project focused on energy policies and technology transfer in the following five areas: clean coal (such as carbon capture and storage and improving the efficiency of power generation); sustainable biofuels, renewable energy, and energy efficiency (buildings, industrial products, and industrial manufacture); and a sustainable and efficient energy allocation system. Training courses, public lectures, conferences, and workshops are organised to archive the above objectives.[41]

Near Zero Emission Coal project (from 2006 onward)

In 2006, the Near Zero Emission Coal (NZEC) project was launched under the framework of the EU and China Partnership on Climate Change to develop carbon dioxide capture and storage (CCS) technology in China.[42] The EU-China Partnership on Climate Change was designed to improve energy efficiency and achieve a low-carbon economy through cooperation on technology. Both sides agreed to take concrete actions to develop, deploy, and lower the cost of clean energy technologies. Through the NZEC project, China and the EU have attempted to develop advanced near-zero-emission coal technology that allows for the capture of CO2 emissions from coal-fired power plants. The major participants in this project are the EC, the UK, and MOST.

China-EU Institute for Clean and Renewable Energy (from 2010 onward)

In 2010, China and the EU co-funded the China-EU Institute for Clean and Renewable Energy (ICARE), located at Huazhong University of Science and

---

40. EC2, 'Know More about EC2', EC2, 2014, http://www.ec2.org.cn/.
41. Ibid.
42. European Commission, 'Questions and Answers on the Communication on Demonstrating Carbon Capture and Geological Storage (CCS) in Emerging Developing Countries: Financing the EU-China Near Zero Emissions Coal Plant Project', European Commission, 2009, https://ec.europa.eu/commission/presscorner/detail/es/MEMO_09_295.

Technology.[43] It is composed of three components: a master's programme in renewable energy, a training centre for energy professionals, and a research support platform. It is expected to provide a platform for international cooperation in energy research.

Other China-EU cooperation projects

There are numerous other ad hoc energy cooperation projects and a series of energy-related conferences, workshops, and joint research projects between China and the EU. Under the EU-China Energy Dialogue, energy cooperation has commenced in multiple fields, such as renewable energy, smart grids, energy efficiency in the building sector, clean coal, nuclear energy, and energy law.[44] A series of energy-related projects were organised, covering a wide range of topics including energy law, coal mine safety, environmental governance, ecological compensation, renewable energy, and energy security. Apart from cooperation with the EU, China has also been cooperating with individual EU member states on energy issues. For example, Germany is China's strategic partner in the development of electric automobiles, France has been China's long-term partner in nuclear energy, and the UK actively promotes CCS technology and offshore wind power in China.

Multilateralism in EU-China Energy Cooperation

The EU-China energy cooperation has demonstrated that China's energy policy has undergone a conceptual change from focusing merely on supply security to incorporating climate issues, particularly sustainability development and energy technology transfer. This is echoed in both the white papers on China's energy policy in 2007, 2012, and 2020, which addressed environmental concerns, climate change, the market, and a low-carbon economy. These new ideas are also embedded in a number of leadership meetings, initiatives, and joint projects between the EU and China; for instance, the 2010 Joint Statement by MOST and the EC emphasises energy research and innovation cooperation. Similarly, the Science and Technology Agreement, signed in 1998 and renewed in 2004, focuses on innovation in renewable energy. The

---

43. ICARE, 'The ICARE Institute', Institute for Clean and Renewable Energy, 2013, http://www.ce-icare.eu/en/article/26/26-en-the-icare-institute; see also Delegation of the European Union to China, 2012, 'Inauguration of China-EU Institute for Clean and Renewable Energy at Huazhong University of Science and Technology', http://eeas.europa.eu/delegations/china/press_corner/all_news/news/2012/20121030_en.htm.
44. European Commission, 'EU-China Cooperation on Energy Issues', European Commission, 2021, https://energy.ec.europa.eu/topics/international-cooperation/key-partner-countries-and-regions/china_en#the-annual-energy-dialogue; PRC NEA, 'Cooperation between China and EU Countries in the Field of Energy', PRC NEA, 2020, https://obor.nea.gov.cn/pictureDetails.html?id=2751.

China-EU Partnership on Climate Change in 2005 included numerous cooperative initiatives on clean energy technology. Projects such as NZEC, EC2, and ICARE are devoted to environmental protection and technology transfer with clean energy cooperation. The EU-China energy cooperation has witnessed an expansion of the idea of energy security from the traditional security of acquiring a supply for the national economic capability to the non-traditional security of environmental issues and technology. Most importantly, the idea behind these projects and initiatives means that both Chinese and European authorities are in principle open to multilateral forms of cooperation.

In the China-EU energy cooperation, both sides have launched several initiatives, ranging from large commercial energy partnerships to joint university educational programmes. In the mid-2000s, both sides established bodies to facilitate multilateral cooperation through a number of joint research projects to facilitate technology transfer. For example, the Joint EEP in 2004, the NZEC project in 2006, the Europe-China Clean Energy Centre (EC2), and China-EU ICARE in 2010 established a platform for China's governmental departments, companies, and institutes to cooperate with the EU, as an integrated entity, or the government of each Member State or the companies and academic institutes based in them.

Although there are high-level channels set up to promote clean energy cooperation between China and the EU member states, both sides have made limited progress in utilising the platforms as a more multilateral means for energy cooperation. There are four reasons why the mechanism of China-EU energy cooperation remains ineffective.

Lack of mutual consensus about R&D practice

A lack of mutual consensus between European and Chinese companies around R&D is a key obstacle in the EU-China energy cooperation.[45] Compared to many international companies with stricter compliance practice, Chinese companies tend to be less attentive towards the practice R&D in general.[46] It appears that China is expecting a 'magic button' that can help fill the tech gap instantly. This expectation difference results in European hesitation in transferring advanced technology to Chinese companies. Energy technology companies, especially smaller ones with a revenue model relying on one or two unique technologies, are particularly concerned about how to protect their assets. Furthermore, some of the aforementioned China-EU energy initiatives have only a short mandate and do not have extension plans after the initial funding stage. This reflects that the Chinese authorities and its European counterpart did not manage to develop a long term project plan which is crucial to

---

45. A former officer at China-Europe joint clean energy center, interview with the author, 2013.
46. Ibid.

R&D. Fragmented coordination structure and administrative burdens have resulted in delays in R&D cooperation.

Trade friction in China-EU clean energy cooperation

Trade frictions and restricted market access have hindered China-EU energy cooperation, especially the flow of technology.[47] In recent years, China has emerged as a new force in solar, wind, and other clean energy sectors, and there has also been a rapid increase in the output of renewable energy equipment and products. Chinese energy companies have undoubtedly risen as a competitor of European enterprises, which have a traditional advantage in the clean energy sector. Low-end and high-end Chinese products entering Europe have also resulted in growing dispute over ESG standards. For example, in 2013, the EU announced provisional anti-dumping and anti-subsidy duties imposed on Chinse imports of solar panels.[48] It was partially a result of EU's growing need to protect its own industry.[49]

Geopolitical tensions over supply chains of critical minerals

Increased geopolitical tensions between the EU and China have contributed to Brussel's mounting concerns about the critical raw materials supply chains. In an EU Commission document entitled *EU-China—A Strategic Outlook* presented in March 2019, the EU labelled China as a 'systemic rival' in some areas.[50] More recently, the EU's coordinated sanctions on Chinese officials have led to further deterioration in their relationships. Consequently, the motion to freeze discussions of the EU-China Comprehensive Agreement on Investment was passed by a landslide vote in the EU.

Geopolitical tension has driven the EU to rethink the supply security of critical raw minerals because these materials are essential to green technology,[51] and China accounts for over 60% of the EU's supply.[52] In particular, the supply

---

47. Michele Knodt and Nadine Piefer, *Challenges of European External Energy Governance with Emerging Powers* (Surrey: Ashgate, 2015), 129–138.
48. European Parliament, 'Making solar a source of EU energy security', European Parliament, 2022, https://www.europarl.europa.eu/RegData/etudes/ATAG/2022/733587/EPRS_ATA(2022)733587_EN.pdf.
49. Katinka Barysch, Charles Grant, and Mark Leonard, 'Embracing the Dragon: Can the EU and China be Friends?' *CESifo Forum* 6, no. 3 (2005): 8–15.
50. European Commission, 'European Commission and HR/VP Contribution to the European Council: EU-China—A Strategic Outlook', European Commission, 2019, https://ec.europa.eu/info/sites/default/files/communication-eu-china-a-strategic-outlook.pdf.
51. The critical raw materials security is crucial to the EU's transition towards a green economy because they are closely linked to clean technologies, such as the batteries used in electric cars.
52. Kaho Yu, 'Critical Minerals Strategy of Asia-Pacific Countries: Diversification, Circular Economy and Multilateral Initiatives', in *Geoeconomics of Decarbonisation in Asia Pacific*, ed.

of rare earth metals has raised additional concerns within the EU due to the dominance of Chinese state-run companies in their production. Aware of the economic importance as well as supply risks of critical raw materials, the European Commission presented the paper *Critical Raw Materials Resilience: Charting a Path towards Greater Security and Sustainability* in September 2020. Moreover, the European Commission announced the creation of the European Raw Materials Alliance.[53] At the heart of these efforts lies the EU's commitment to strengthening its strategic independence and becoming carbon-neutral by 2050, potentially limiting the scope of cooperation with China.

Divergence in core values and policy priorities

When confronted with a range of governance issues in either traditional or non-traditional security, China and the EU generally have limited room working together, as they hold different core assumptions.[54] For example, China and the EU have different priorities and paces for their own climate agenda, resulting in frequent disagreements; for example, their different views towards the pace of energy transition. For example, China's latest plans reaffirmed that coal will remain the country's key choice for power generation over the next decade because renewables are not yet ready as a replacement, despite the large-scale development of wind and solar power. China also appears to be reluctant to fully rely on WTO as a way to settle trade disputes with the EU in the clean energy sector.

In sum, it is difficult to effectively implement the multilateral energy cooperation between China and the EU via existing platforms and programmes due to the above obstacles. It has further driven China to rely on its conventional bilateral approach, given that it already has a clear view of the exact partners that are suitable for particular projects.[55] Engaging with a group of diversified stakeholders separately gives China various options for its cooperation target and allows it to enjoy better leverage in negotiations. This also allows China to maximise its advantages by switching between multilateral China-EU cooperation and bilateral China-EU Member State cooperation.[56] Moreover, while different EU Member States have their own specific strengths

---

KAS (Berlin: Konrad-Adenauer-Stiftung, 2022), 8–27.
53. European Commission, 'Critical Raw Materials Resilience: Charting a Path towards Greater Security and Sustainability', European Commission, 2020, https://eur-lex.europa.eu/legal-content/EN/TXT/HTML/?uri=CELEX:52020DC0474&from=EN.
54. David Kerr and Yanzhou Xu, 'Europe, China, and Security Governance: Is There Evidence of Normative Convergence?' *Asia Europe Journal* 12, no. 1–2 (2012): 79–93.
55. Daojiong Zha and Suetyi Lai, 'EU-China Energy Governance: What Lessons to Be Drawn?', in *Challenges of European External Energy Governance with Emerging Powers*, ed. Michele Knodt and Nadine Piefer (Surrey: Ashgate, 2015), 129–138.
56. Ibid.

and business interests with regard to renewable energy,[57] China has also formulated different diplomatic strategies with individual European partners for particular projects. Flexibility and effectiveness are other reasons why China prefers bilateral agreements with EU Member States. In state-to-state deals, China finds it easier to proceed with concrete actions. This pragmatic approach hinders the level of Chinese participation in multilateral channels. As a result, although there are multilateral forms of cooperation and high-level exchanges between China and the EU, progress remains limited.

---

57. For example, France in nuclear electricity, Germany in photovoltaic power generation, Denmark in wind power, etc.

6
Conclusion

What Is Next for China in Global Energy Governance?

Chinese energy security has traditionally been associated with a political-economic approach, but supply disruptions due to geopolitics and climate change over the past two decades have driven China to promote global energy governance as a way to enhance its energy security. The year of 2006–2007 was a turning point, when China began to adopt a more balanced energy strategy that reflected this shift. Oil price fluctuation, global financial crisis, and climate risks drove China to look into global governance as a means to enhance its energy security. Since then, China has been engaged in many multilateral platforms and international organisations for energy cooperation. In the 2010s, the BRI and Paris Agreement added extra momentum to China's participation in global energy governance. There has been a long debate over to what extent China's international energy behaviour has shifted to a more global governance approach.

The discussion of multilateral energy cooperation as a means to enhance energy security first appeared in the white papers of 2007 on China's foreign affairs and energy policy. The Chinese government emphasised the concept of global energy governance in its white paper on energy in 2012 and 2020, policy documents of the BRI, and action plans for carbon reduction. These acts reflect how the Chinese leadership has changed its understanding of energy security towards multilateral energy cooperation and global energy governance.

However, while calling for global energy governance, Chinese authorities have also shown a mixed attitude towards international organisations led by rivals. A common viewpoint shared among Chinese scholars and political elites is that China should follow its own development path instead of blindly joining a Western-led international organisation. While there is no urgent need to join existing international organisations, China has started creating its own multilateral platforms and rules for energy cooperation, particularly under the BRI. This chapter summarises the multilateral practices of China's international energy cooperation in the following four case studies.

Conclusion

Belt and Road Initiative and the Asia Infrastructure Investment Bank

The BRI has turned China's engagement in Eurasia into a multilateral engagement strategy that has tapped into global governance via China-led institutes such as the AIIB. The AIIB is the first MDB to have a majority of members from developing countries. With both geo-economic and geopolitical dimensions, energy cooperation in the BRI intends to spur Eurasian connectivity by using the AIIB's massive potential for investment. Aligning with the Vision and Actions on Energy Cooperation, energy investment in the AIIB has emphasised the interconnectivity of infrastructures, sustainable development, and the mobilisation of private capital.

The AIIB reflects the willingness of China to institutionalise its participate in global energy governance, and has allowed China to enjoy primary leadership in an international organisation with substantial economic involvement in the global South amid growing climate pressures. Moreover, a broad membership base, including both developing and developed countries, brings the AIIB a solid reputation, legitimacy, and new agenda-setting power because it can ensure that the bank follows standards such as accountability, transparency, and governance.[1] Under the umbrella of multilateralism—with Western governments such as the UK as key members of the AIIB—it is difficult for the bank to deviate from the norms, rules, and practices of such governments support.

Since the regions under the BRI contain significant divergences in operational and investment risks, the AIIB energy projects shown in Appendix Table 1—which involve cross-border or multinational issues, such as cross-border transmission, transition of energy, interest distribution, responsibility, and national sovereignty—can be exposed to investment delays or disputes. A 2015 report from the Brookings Institute highlighted that "Chinese investment is equally distributed between good and poor (i.e., riskier) governance environments, whereas Western investment is concentrated in the former."[2] Thus, it is necessary to create a web of investment-treaty protections overlying the route to provide a crucial means of reducing the risks involved in the investment.

However, China has attempted to avoid over-participation in restrictive treaties established by the West and has been reluctant to accept certain requirements imposed on members in these organisations.[3] Instead, establish-

---

1. John Gerard Ruggie, *Multilateralism Matters: The Theory and Praxis of an Institutional Form* (New York: Columbia University Press, 1993).
2. Weijie Chen, David Dollar, and Heiwai Tang, 'Why Is China Investing in Africa? Evidence from the Firm Level', *The World Bank Economic Review* 32, no. 3 (2018): 610–632.
3. For example, China remains an observer of the Energy Charter partly because a full membership requires the ratification of the Energy Charter Treaty (ECT), which could involve potential political risks. In other words, China wants to remain unobligated and to be able to 'exit' whenever it feels it is necessary to do so. The Chinese authorities were alarmed by the 2014 Yukos lawsuit filed under the ECT against the Russian government. The authorities

ing a new institution would allow China to have a greater influence in global governance of energy and climate issue and to establish its own standards for future investment and trade. If the AIIB offers more competitive and permissive loans than the Western creditors, developing countries that are not able to meet the criteria of these creditors may turn to the AIIB. In the face of the competition imposed by China and the AIIB, the norms, rules, and practices of existing financing system may be undermined in the long run.

China–Central Asia Energy Cooperation

Given its strategic location, China views Central Asia as a key partner in its 'going-out' strategy and the BRI. Their relationship is mainly driven by China's need to diversify energy supplies and security goals to create an 'amicable, secure and prosperous neighbourhood'.[4] China's top leaders attempted to promote China–Central Asia energy cooperation via diplomatic means, such as strengthening relations with Central Asian countries and supporting the activities of Chinese NOCs in Central Asia. While energy diplomacy is believed to have renewed the momentum of Chinese energy cooperation with Central Asia, joint energy infrastructure has also strengthened the energy ties between China and these regions.

The Central Asia–China transnational pipeline announced in 2007 is considered one of the most outstanding achievements in China's energy cooperation with Central Asia that has structurally changed how China works with Central Asian countries. This transnational gas pipeline is China's first and largest cross-border gas pipeline that has tied China with its Central Asian partners in an infrastructure network and long-term supply contracts. Moreover, it has laid the foundation for multilateralism because the need for transnational transit management has encouraged China to look into better energy governance from a multilateral approach. This prospect is further reflected in the attention paid by Chinese authorities to the potential for a multilateral regulatory platform such as ECT in protecting Chinese NOCs' interests in the region.

SCO appeared to be an ideal platform for China and its Central Asian partners to manage the transnational pipeline and their broader energy cooperation. Indeed, since 2003, over 100 energy projects have been placed under SCO, with a series of agreements regarding multilateral energy cooperation being signed. The construction of a Central Asia–China pipeline in addition to Russia's proposal of establishing an 'Energy Club' in 2006 reignited Chinese

---

thus paid attention to the risk of signing the ECT rather than how the ECT could protect the investment or the company. The authorities expressed concern about whether the Chinese government might be exposed to similar potential lawsuits that were faced by the Russian government.
4. Zhaoxing Li, 'Peace, Development and Cooperation—Banner for China's Diplomacy in the New Era', *Chinese Journal of International Law* 4, no. 2 (2005): 677–683.

interest in using SCO as a multilateral platform to promote energy cooperation. However, due to a lack of effective legal mechanisms in the SCO, the actual implementation of energy projects among its member states remained bilateral. Operational risks of large infrastructure projects will still drive China to explore more effective coordination mechanisms with Central Asian countries, but that will require significant diplomatic effect, substantial financial resources, and years of time.

China-Africa Energy Cooperation

Driven by China's increasing need to reduce its oil dependency on the Middle East, the China-Africa energy cooperation began to expand in the early 1990s, and eventually became a key aspect in China's 'going-out' strategy and the BRI. Although oil and gas projects have predominantly characterised China's energy engagement with African countries over the last three decades, China's signing of the Paris Agreement has gradually shifted its cooperation towards a more climate and sustainability centred one. Despite being a latecomer to Africa, China has its advantages in establishing an energy relationship with African countries, including China's effort in promoting of South-South cooperation.

While Chinese NOCs have taken the initiative to expand investment in Africa, top leadership meetings and bilateral ties have also been a key means to promote China-Africa energy cooperation. In 2006, a pan-African approach was proposed in China's African Policy, which aimed to 'encourage and support competent Chinese enterprises to cooperate with African nations . . . to develop and exploit rationally their resources'.[5] The policy paved the way for promoting energy and climate cooperation in a more multilateral way—FOCAC, a joint ministerial conference held every three years to cultivate a long-term China-Africa relationship with solidarity and cooperation. Through FOCAC, China has attempted to facilitate market access, optimise trade structures, promote green development, offer aid, and settle trade disputes. FOCAC also provides multilateral consultation and coordination mechanisms with which China and Africa can handle practical situations. More importantly, FOCAC is established and led by developing countries and serves as a multilateral platform for South-South cooperation.

However, implementation of plans agreed in FOCAC is not always effective. First, although the FOCAC meetings issued documents with follow-up plans to facilitate multilateral cooperation between China and Africa, the details for actions are not elaborated. It is difficult for either side to implement the policies and visions originating from the Forum successfully. Second, FOCAC lacks a well-organised and legal structure to facilitate or protect

---

5. PRC State Council, 'Government Issues African Policy Paper', PRC State Council, 2006, http://www.gov.cn/misc/2006-01/12/content_156509.htm.

China's energy investment in Africa. Many of the agreements were only signed as a guidance of governments. Third, Chinese authorities consider bilateral cooperation to be more effective in the China-Africa energy cooperation and tend to rely on it. Therefore, while FOCAC can serve as a channel for Chinese energy diplomacy, the Forum appears to be used to strengthen bilateral ties.

China-EU Clean Energy Cooperation

The EU has a unique role in China's energy strategy due to its leading experience in climate solution and clean energy innovation. The signature of the Paris Agreement and the need to tackle climate change have further driven the pair to promote clean energy cooperation. This partnership has become an important means for China to enhance its energy security by focusing on energy transition. It has demonstrated that China's energy policy has undergone a conceptual change from focusing merely on supply security to incorporating climate issues, particularly sustainability development and energy technology transfer.

To advance their energy cooperation, China and the EU have established official dialogues, such as the China-EU Energy Conference, the China-Europe High-Level Energy Working Group, the China-Europe Energy Dialogue, and the EU-China Summit. Over the past two decades, these official dialogues have covered a wide range of energy issues, particularly climate change, sustainable development, and clean energy cooperation. China and the EU have also launched a number of joint energy programmes to promote personnel exchange and training, technology transfer, and joint R&D and financial investment in the energy industry.[6]

Although there are high-level channels set up to promote clean energy cooperation between China and the EU Member States, both sides have made limited progress in utilising the platforms as a more multilateral means for energy cooperation. While China appears to prefer engaging with EU member states separately to enjoy better leverage in negotiations, there are four reasons why the mechanism of China-EU energy cooperation remains ineffective. First, there is a lack of consensus about R&D practice in the broader China-EU business relationship. Short project mandate, fragmented coordination structure and administrative burdens have also resulted in delays in R&D cooperation. Second, trade frictions in multiple areas, from solar panel to market access, have hindered China-EU cooperation. Low-end and high-end Chinese products entering Europe have also resulted in increasing competition and growing dispute over ESG standards. Third, growing geopolitical tension has complicated the broader China-EU relationship, including the prospect of the EU-China Comprehensive Agreement on Investment. Increasing tension has

---

6. Such as Joint Energy and Environment Programme in 2004, the NZEC project in 2006, the Europe-China Clean Energy Centre EC2, and the China-EU ICARE in 2010.

particularly driven the EU to rethink the security of its critical mineral supply, which is essential to cleantech innovation and simultaneously relies heavily on China. Fourth, divergence in values and policy priorities, such as the pace of energy transition, is another obstacle to cooperation.

Four Challenges China Faces in Global Energy Governance

New institutions in the BRI, a transnational pipeline with Central Asia, strategy in China-Africa energy cooperation, and EU-China clean energy cooperation has demonstrated China's increasing willingness to use global governance to deal with energy and climate issues. A series of policy documents, action plans, and investments reflect that the Chinese government has incorporated new elements from global governance to climate issues into the consideration of energy security. This policy evolution from energy diplomacy to a strategy that incorporates global energy governance has raised the question about the extent to which China would work with multilateralism.

A policy change can be understood as 'a dramatic departure in policy goals, based on a new theoretical and ideological framework'.[7] It can occur when there is a crisis representing shock or insecurity for which the authorities must decisively intervene. The understanding of crisis refers to a moment of an abrupt change in external circumstance that can lead to 'decisive intervention' to establish new objectives and new policy instruments.[8] In the context of energy, the Fukushima incident, extreme climates, and the abrupt cut of the Russian gas supply to Europe are considered 'crises' that have resulted in policy paradigm shifts. Notably, the processes of change are not necessarily linear or clean-cut, and instead, can be messy and contingent. The change in a policy paradigm shift can be revolutionary or evolutionary depending on the continuity, pace, and degree of change. The shift can occur over time, and an evolutionary change can lead to a revolutionary change.

All cases in this research show that Chinese authorities have incorporated new ideas of multilateral cooperation or global governance in their rationale underlying China's energy and climate strategy. They have also introduced new policy instruments and goals in response to the growing need for global energy governance. When the BRI was introduced, the Chinese government also established the AIIB to facilitate investments. In the China–Central Asia energy cooperation, while joint energy projects were expanded, such as transnational pipelines including multilateral parties, SCO was introduced as a

---

7. Peter Hall, 'Policy Paradigms, Social Learning and the State: The Case of Economic Policymaking in Britain', *Comparative Politics* 25 (1993): 275–297.
8. Colin Hay, 'The "Crisis" of Keynesianism and the Rise of Neoliberalism in Britain: An Ideational Institutionalist Approach', in *The Rise of Neoliberalism and Institutional Analysis*, ed. John L. Campbell and Ove K. Pedersen (Princeton, NJ: Princeton University Press, 2001), 193–218; Dieter Helm, 'The New Energy Paradigm', in *The New Energy Paradigm*, ed. Dieter Helm (Oxford: Oxford University Press, 2007), 9.

multilateral platform to coordinate energy cooperation. In the China-Africa energy cooperation, FOCAC was introduced as a multilateral platform to coordinate energy cooperation. In the EU-China energy cooperation, more energy initiatives, including joint projects and joint centres, were established under the EU framework.

However, the level of implementation of these instruments and their goals can vary and undermine their legitimacy as well as the underlying rationales. Chapters 3, 4, and 5 indicate that although there were new cooperation institutions, platforms, and/or joint projects in China's multilateral cooperation with Central Asia, Africa, and the EU, the extent of the implementation was ineffective or limited. The effectiveness of these multilateral mechanisms was low because the involved parties lacked the willingness and urgency to make a change. Incompetence in the instruments reflected that the underlying rationale of establishing these platforms still depended on the traditional approach—at least, and the changes (i.e., crisis) have not been sufficient to justify them as a 'dramatic departure'.

The AIIB is an outlier. It was set up with a new set of principles and management culture, which is similar to well-established institutions like the World Bank and IMF. It is also the first multinational development bank to have a majority of members from developing countries. With both geo-economic and geopolitical dimensions, energy cooperation in the BRI is meant to boost Eurasian connectivity by using the AIIB's massive potential for investment. Aligning with the Vision and Actions on Energy Cooperation, energy investment in the AIIB has emphasised the interconnectivity of infrastructures, sustainable development, and the mobilisation of private capital. The AIIB reflects the appropriation and legitimacy of China's claim to participate in global energy governance and has allowed China to enjoy primary leadership in an international organisation with substantial economic involvement in the global South. As such, the AIIB demonstrates substantial changes in the instrument, goal, and rationale that China has moved towards multilateralism.

These findings do not fully align with the pledges made in China's energy white papers or the BRI (see Chapter 1 and 2). In particular, the white papers in 2007, 2012, and 2020 and the official documents of the BRI address the importance of and China's effort in multilateral approaches to international energy cooperation. They reflect that there was an inconsistency between policy planning and implementation in China's energy security. There are at least four challenges as to why a policy change to incorporate multilateralism in Chinese energy security was not carried out effectively, despite calls by Chinese authorities for good global energy governance.

Challenge 1: Fragmented Chinese energy governance

China has a fragmented energy governance structure, with constant reforms, decentralisation, and bureaucratic ineffectiveness. Over twenty government bodies and major SOEs have overlapping functions and responsibilities in China's energy governance structure. The authority over China's energy sector is decentralised to different actors, and the disintegration of policymaking is unavoidable. A policy can be made by several government sectors and carried out by different actors. The formulation and implementation of energy policy have become a process in which different parties struggle and compete for interests. Moreover, central authorities are not always resourceful enough to control and manage the entire energy industry; therefore, local operations rely on the local governments. The same logic applies to the central authorities' influence over Chinese NOCs that operate abroad. High-level guidelines may not always align with considerations in actual operations. As a result, ineffectiveness in energy governance hinders the implementation of energy policy.

Challenge 2: Mis-expectation of multilateralism

A common viewpoint shared by Chinese authorities is that China should follow its own development path rather than a Western one. Such a statement implies that there could be an 'ideological gap' between the West and China in how they understand global energy governance and China's role in it. While multilateralism or global energy governance entails the establishment of an institution and enforcement of rules, it could be difficult for China to fully align with controversial requirements set by rivals. This gap is reflected in China's attitudes towards joining treaty organisations, such as the Energy Charter Treaty (see Chapter 2), and addressing global agendas such as ESG practices and the pace of energy transition (see Chapter 5).

Challenge 3: A lack of urgent needs

Decisive intervention to make a policy change is always triggered by a crisis. For example, high oil prices in the mid-2000s drove China to discuss multilateral cooperation as a way to stabilise the energy markets. Similarly, due to the impact of the 2008 global financial crisis on energy markets, China called for global energy governance. Increasing climate risks have also pushed China to incorporate global climate cooperation and energy transition into its energy policy. In other words, due to increasing external pressures, Chinese authorities recognise the importance of integration into the global energy cooperation system and comprehensive measures to ensure energy security. However, the case of Turkmenistan gas export disruption (see Chapter 3) indicates that it would be no urgent need to trigger a material policy change if there had not been a crisis of sufficient severity.

Challenge 4: Lengthy process of evolutionary policy change

The processes of change are not necessarily revolutionary, but instead, could be evolutionary. Change is not always linear or clean cut, and can be dynamic and contingent. Therefore, the process of change from bilateralism to multilateralism takes time. This research indicates that bilateral approaches could be more efficient and flexible for Chinese authorities. With fewer parties involved, coordination costs are lower and there is clarity of interest. Moreover, there are different histories, cultures, domestic politics, and economic development levels in different regions, which a bilateral approach can address more directly.[9] As a result, a bilateral approach has remained a core part of China's international energy cooperation, even after multilateral approaches are introduced. Instead, multilateralism is more of a tool for China to counter and benefit from the existing liberal system. In the short to mid-term, China will likely continue to use multilateralism as a hedging strategy to maximise opportunities. 'National interests seem to explain much of China's devotion to multilateralism or, where relevant, the lack thereof'.[10]

Despite the above challenges, all cases in this research indicated that China has not closed its doors to multilateralism, as presented in China's interests in the existing international institutions, willingness to initiate new institutions, and the growing importance of transnational infrastructure. In the long term, these multilateral elements will drive China to look more closely at global energy governance. However, there is no magic button for policy change and this process could last for years or decades and could even result in a new development path.

What Is Next?

China is at an important juncture in its approach towards global energy governance. On one hand, it is widely seen as a solution provider to address emerging issues from market disruptions to climate change. On the other, its role in global energy governance is facing growing geopolitical challenges. The overlap between diplomatic and economic issues results in a cycle of retaliatory actions, from trade/investment restrictions to coordinated sanctions.

---

9. Janice Heppell, 'Confidence-Building Measures: Bilateral versus Multilateral Approaches', in *Peace and Security in Northeast Asia: The Nuclear Issue and the Korean Peninsula*, ed. Young Whan Kihl and Peter Hayes (Armonk, NY: M E Sharpe, 1997), 269–301.
10. Jean-Marc F. Blanchard, 'Harmonious World and China's Foreign Economic Policy: Features, Implications, and Challenges', *Journal of Chinese Political Science* 13, no. 3 (2008): 165–192, 174.

Conclusion

The COVID-19 pandemic has further complicated both the global market and diplomatic relations. There are also growing international pressures on China to accelerate its energy transition. While China is adopting a more assertive foreign policy due to its growing global interests, fundamental differences in market principles and democratic values have fuelled the geopolitical tensions between China and the West. All these emerging factors have driven China to reinforce its strategy to be self-reliant in the global supply chain. It is set to expand its global economic and political influence and assume a more proactive role in global governance.

The establishment of the AIIB reflects China's hesitation to rely solely on existing international organisations led by the West, such as the World Bank, the Asian Development Bank, the Energy Charter, etc. Instead, China has learnt from its experience with these organisations and advocated that the AIIB can develop both competitive and cooperative relationships with existing institutes, thereby reshaping the political and economic dynamics among several Eurasian regions. China is not only affected by global energy governance, but its behaviour towards multilateralism will also result in geopolitical implications. The BRI, together with institutions such as the AIIB, can potentially enhance China's global role through the following pathway.

Devolution from the existing multilateral financing system

While the AIIB allows China to enjoy primary leadership in an international organisation with substantial economic involvement in Eurasia, it also presents a possible 'exit' option for China to devolve from existing institutes. The AIIB is another example of 'devolution away from the centralised global economic institutions created at Bretton Woods in 1944 and towards a more regional framework'.[11] According to Morse and Keohane's concept of 'contested multilateralism', when there is dissatisfaction with existing institutions, new institutes will be created to challenge the rules, practices, or missions of existing multilateral institutions.[12] The AIIB offers China an alternative pathway to accommodate itself in the multilateral development lending system as well as global energy governance.[13] According to the ADB, in order to maintain the development momentum in Asia, US$26 trillion will be required from 2016 to

---

11. Stephen Grenville, 'The Asian Infrastructure Investment Bank and the Rise of Regionalism', Lowy Institute, 2015, https://www.lowyinstitute.org/the-interpreter/asian-infrastructure-investment-bank-and-rise-regionalism.
12. Julia Morse Robert Keohane, 'Contested multilateralism', *Review of International Organizations* 9, no. 4 (2014): 385–412.
13. Economist, 'Why China Is Creating a New "World Bank" for Asia', *Economist*, 11 November 2014, https://www.economist.com/blogs/economist-explains/2014/11/economist-explains-6.

2030.[14] It is difficult for existing institutes, including the World Bank and the ADB, to fill in that funding gap and still leave room for new institutes such as the AIIB.[15] There is also a widespread perception among developing countries that the existing MDBs require reform because of their inefficient and bureaucratic lending systems.

It is not necessary for the AIIB to end the Bretton Woods agreement or replace the World Bank or the ADB.[16] Instead, considering the demand for infrastructural investment in Asia, the AIIB can play a complementary role alongside other financial institutions. As Appendix Table 1 indicates, most of the AIIB's energy projects were co-financed with other financial institutions, including the World Bank, the ADB, the European Bank for Reconstruction and Development, and the European Investment Bank. The AIIB has also signed cooperation agreements with the World Bank and the ADB to work together in the areas of energy, transportation, telecommunications, development, and climate mitigation.[17] Throughout these arrangements, the AIIB and China can learn from existing multilateral systems and modify and apply certain aspects of their structures to their own systems. New institutions may cooperate or compete with existing institutions. In China's interactions with existing international energy organisations, the nation (as of 2018) enjoys the upper hand in the negotiations. Thus, these organisations are willing to modify their own agendas to accommodate China. This scenario has provided room for China to modify the current order with its own strategic preferences.

New interconnection with asymmetric interdependency

The BRI has brought the AIIB and its combined commercial strategies and developmental policies to the targeted region, creating a new pattern of alliance. Over time, increasing energy investment under the AIIB will advance regional economic integration and increase the region's economic reliance on China.[18] The Chinese government emphasised in 2015 that strengthen-

---

14. ADB, 'Meeting Asia's Infrastructure Needs', ADB, 2017, https://www.adb.org/publications/asia-infrastructure-needs.
15. AIIB, 'Energy Sector Strategy: Sustainable Energy for Asia', Asian Infrastructure Investment Bank, 2017, https://www.aiib.org/en/policies-strategies/strategies/sustainable-energy-asia/index.html.
16. David Dollar, 'China as a Global Investor' (Working Paper 4, Brookings Institute, 2016), G.-F. Legault, 'AIIB Melding, Not Moulding Global Governance', East Asia Forum, 2015, http://www.eastasiaforum.org/2015/11/18/aiib-melding-not-moulding-global-governance.
17. ADB, 'ADB, AIIB Sign MOU to Strengthen Cooperation for Sustainable Growth', ADB, 2016, https://www.adb.org/news/adb-aiib-sign-mou-strengthen-cooperation-sustainable-growth; World Bank, 'World Bank and AIIB Sign Cooperation Framework', World Bank, 2017, https://www.worldbank.org/en/news/press-release/2017/04/23/world-bank-and-aiib-sign-cooperation-framework.
18. Bonnie Glaser, 'China's Grand Strategy in Asia', CSIS, 2014, https://csis-website-prod.s3.amazonaws.com/s3fs-public/legacy_files/files/attachments/ts140313_glaser.pdf.

ing energy cooperation in the BRI can 'stimulate wider and deeper regional cooperation at a higher level for the economic prosperity of the whole world'[19] and that 'the core of the international industrial cooperation is to encourage [China's] advanced capacity to go global'.[20] Indeed, the BRI is not the first initiative to promote interconnection via investment in a region. For instance, the European experience with Trans-European Energy Networks (TEN-E)[21] has shown clear synergies between infrastructure networks and the market in Europe. While TEN-E could satisfy energy demand for economic and industrial development, it also contributed to implementing the EU's primary policies, including integrating markets, connecting regions, and increasing social cohesion.[22]

In the BRI, energy investment via the AIIB is not merely a matter of securing energy supply, but also part of a regional integration plan. As indicated in Appendix Table 1, the AIIB's energy investments are all found in developing regions, where such investments address challenges in energy access, development, and climate change. The sufficient interconnection of infrastructure, especially in remote regions, can stimulate economic growth and development. Other than energy supply, energy investment in the AIIB will contribute to market creation, development, and energy transition in regions from South Asia to the Middle East. Economic development and integration are both important for the BRI in addressing the wide range of challenges China faces, including slumping economic growth, domestic overcapacity and overproduction, backward development in western China, as well as political and security instability in 'neighbourhood' regions.[23] The Chinese government believes that the development opportunities emerging from the BRI and the AIIB can help stabilise these regions.[24]

---

19. PRC NDRC, PRC MFA, and PRC MOFCOM, 'Vision and Actions on Jointly Building the Silk Road Economic Belt and the 21st-Century Maritime Silk Road', PRC NDRC, 2015, https://www.fmprc.gov.cn/eng/topics_665678/2015zt/xjpcxbayzlt2015nnh/201503/t20150328_705553.html.
20. Xinhua News, 'China Not Seeking to Move Outdated Capacity Abroad', *Xinhua News*, 20 May 2015, http://www.china.org.cn/business/2015-05/20/content_35617344.htm.
21. TEN-E is part of a wider system of Trans-European Networks (TENs). In TEN-E, various European regions and national networks are linked by the creation of modern and effective infrastructures. European experience has shown that the connection in energy infrastructures not only benefits energy transfer in particular sectors, but also supports the creation of a competitive market, to the benefit of industrial and private consumers. In the long run, such connectivity helps to integrate the economies in the whole region.
22. Tomas Maltby, 'European Union Energy Policy Integration: A Case of European Commission Policy Entrepreneurship and Increasing Supranationalism', *Energy Policy* 55 (2013): 435–444.
23. Lucy Hornby, 'China Seeks Foreign Investors for One Belt, One Road Push', *Financial Times*, 25 May 2016; Dragan Pavlićević, 'China, the EU and One Belt, One Road Strategy', *China Brief* 15, no. 15 (2015), http://www.jamestown.org/programs/chinabrief/single/?tx_ttnews%5Btt_news%5D=44235&cHash=9dbc08472c19ecd691307c4c1905eb0c#.V9-58CTuCXs.
24. Beijing believes that an economic slowdown in the 'neighbourhood', especially Central and South Asia, will result in social and security instability, both of which can further harm

In an integrated system, however, multi-layered power can result in potential conflicts between national sovereignty and various projects. Key decisions on cross-border energy projects are typically made on the basis of national priorities. Similarly, costs and benefits are asymmetric among countries in the BRI.[25] Based on the BRI's principle of mutual benefits, energy projects within the BRI should be of common interest and have net socioeconomic benefits. An energy project can be favourable from the BRI's perspective, but not from an individual country's perspective. In some cases, an energy project can be favourable from an individual country's perspective, but may achieve few socio-economic benefits beyond that country's borders.

Climate and infrastructure in future multilateral engagement

The development of the BRI especially in climate and energy infrastructure cooperation will reshape supply chains and financing in the region. It will increase the region's economic reliance on China and will promote integration between the surrounding regions. Energy investments along the BRI will benefit from the development of a new framework with new methods of resource distribution, value chain integration, green development, logistic network development, and regional governance. As long as the growing demand for BRI-related energy investment exists, large-scale infrastructure projects, such as transnational pipelines, will require multilateral mechanisms to provide investment protection and project management. Considering the investment scale and geographical coverage of the BRI, a more robust multilateral framework is needed to achieve successful energy cooperation under this initiative.

By embracing the traditional Chinese saying, 'To create wealth—first build a road', the Chinese leadership considers connectivity, particularly via transport and energy infrastructure, the key to boosting the development and economy of the region. With strong geo-economic, geopolitical, and climate dimensions, energy cooperation in the BRI is meant to spur Eurasian connectivity by using China's enormous potential for investment and trade. As stated in the Vision and Actions on Energy Cooperation, energy cooperation in the BRI emphasises new market creation, value chain integration, and green development. In the long run, the connectivity of infrastructure in the BRI will reshape multilateral engagement in the region, resulting in a new form of global governance for energy and climate issues.

---

the political stability of Chinese provinces that are close to these regions. Security issues, such as terrorism, separatism, and extremism, in these regions have been a top concern for Beijing.

25. Prashanth Parameswaran, 'The Real Trouble with China's Belt and Road', *The Diplomat*, 11 May 2017, https://thediplomat.com/2017/05/the-real-trouble-with-chinas-belt-and-road/.

Appendix

Table 1: AIIB-Sponsored Energy Projects AIIB (2015–2017)

Project	Location	Borrower	Funding bodies	Fund (USD mil.)
Trans-Anatolian Natural Gas Pipeline Project	Azerbaijan	Southern Gas Corridor Joint Stock Company	AIIB, WB, EIB, EBRD, others	8,600
Distribution System Upgrade and Expansion Project	Bangladesh	Dhaka Electric Supply Company Ltd.	AIIB, others	n/a
Natural Gas Infrastructure and Efficiency Improvement Project	Bangladesh	Bangladesh	AIIB, ADB, Bangladesh gov't	453
Bangladesh Bhola IPP	Bangladesh	Nutan Bidyut Ltd.	AIIB	60
Beijing Air Quality Improvement and Coal Replacement Project	China	Beijing Gas	AIIB, Beijing Municip., China CDM Fund, Beijing Gas	761
Egypt Round II Solar PV Feed-in Tariffs Program	Egypt	Al Subh Solar Power SAE	AIIB, IFC, others	41
280 MW Nenskra Hydropower Plant	Georgia	JSC Nenskra Hydro	AIIB	86.7
Andhra Pradesh 24 × 7—Power for All	India	India	AIIB, WB, Andhra Pradesh gov't	571
Transmission System Strengthening Project (Tamil Nadu)	India	Powergrid	AIIB, ADB, Powergrid	303

Project	Location	Borrower	Funding bodies	Fund (USD mil.)
Myingyan 225 MW Combined Cycle Gas Turbine (CCGT) Power Plant Project	Myanmar	Private	AIIB, ADB, others	20
Tarbela 5th Extension Hydropower Project	Pakistan	Pakistan	AIIB, WB, Pakistan gov't	823
Nurek Hydropower Rehabilitation Project Phase I	Tajikistan	Tajikistan	AIIB, WB, EDB	350
Tuz Golu Gas Storage Expansion Project	Turkey	Boru Hatları İle Petrol Taşıma AŞ	AIIB, WB, Boru Hatları İle Petrol Taşıma AŞ	2500

Source: AIIB.

Appendix

Table 2: Joint Energy Projects of SCO Member States

Project	Participating Countries	Duration	Departments Involved
Energy projects research and implementation among China, Kazakhstan, Russia, and Tajikistan	China, Russia, Kazakhstan, and Tajikistan	2004–2009	Chinese Ministry of Commerce, Tajik Ministry of Economic Development and Trade, and relevant departments of other SCO member countries
Analysis of the prospects of energy fuel complex cooperation for SCO member countries	SCO member countries	2004	Russian Ministry of Industry and Energy, Chinese Ministry of Commerce, Tajik Ministry of Economic Development and Trade, State Energy Company of Uzbekistan, Oil and Gas State-Controlled Companies of Uzbekistan, and relevant departments of other SCO member countries
Proposals of energy cooperation priorities and joint plan and projects of mutual interest	SCO member countries	2004–2007	Russian Ministry of Industry and Energy, Chinese Ministry of Commerce, Tajik Ministry of Economic Development and Trade, State Energy Company of Uzbekistan, Oil and Gas Companies of Uzbekistan, Oil and Gas State-Controlled Companies of Uzbekistan, and relevant departments of other SCO member countries
Study of the possibilities of consistency among standards, technology, and regulations of the current gas transport system	SCO member countries	2004–2006	Russian Ministry of Energy and Industry, Kyrgyzstan's State Assets and Investment Committee, Kyrgyzstan's natural gas company, Tajik Ministry of Energy and Industry, Oil and Gas State-Controlled Companies of Uzbekistan, and relevant departments of other SCO member countries
Co-construction of the hydropower facilities for Kyrgyzstan and Tajikistan	Russia, China, Kyrgyzstan, and Tajikistan	2004–2005	Russian Ministry of Energy and Industry, 'Russian Unified Power System' Company, Kyrgyzstan's State Assets and Investment Committee, Tajik Ministry of Energy, and Industry and relevant departments of Russia and China

Project	Participating Countries	Duration	Departments Involved
Study of the possibilities of expanding the transport capacity of existing natural gas pipelines within Kyrgyzstan	China, Russia, Kazakhstan, Kyrgyzstan, and Tajikistan	2005	Kyrgyzstan's State Assets and Investment Committee, Kyrgyzstan's natural gas company and relevant departments of China, Russia, Kazakhstan, Kyrgyzstan, and Tajikistan
Hydroelectric Power Stations in Kyrgyzstan	China, Russia, and Kyrgyzstan	2004–2005	Russian power companies, Kyrgyzstan power companies, and relevant departments of Russia and China
Study of the questions about creating conditions for mutual access to the electricity market between SCO member countries and barrier-free electricity transit within them	SCO member countries	2004	Kyrgyzstan power companies, State Grid Corporation of Kyrgyzstan, State Energy Company of Uzbekistan, Tajik Ministry of Energy and Industry, and relevant departments of SCO member countries
SCO member countries participating in the development of 500 220-kilovolt mains in Kyrgyzstan and Tajikistan in order to improve transmission capacity	Russia, China, Kyrgyzstan, and Tajikistan	2004–2005	State Grid Corporation of Kyrgyzstan, Tajik Ministry of Energy and Industry, and relevant departments of Russia and China
Information exchange on the reform process of power field markets and the development prospects of the power industry	SCO member countries	Long-term	State Energy Company of Uzbekistan, Tajik Ministry of Energy and Industry, and relevant departments of SCO member countries
SCO member countries participating in the bid invitation of concession of 'Nortel' Distribution Company in Tajikistan	China, Russia, Kazakhstan, Kyrgyzstan, and Tajikistan	2004–2005	'Kyrgyzstan power companies, Tajik Ministry of Energy and Industry and relevant departments of China, Russia, Kazakhstan, Kyrgyzstan, and Tajikistan
Co-construction of Rogun Hydropower Station	Tajikistan, China and Russia	2005–2010	Tajik Ministry of Energy and Industry and relevant departments of China and Russia

Appendix

Project	Participating Countries	Duration	Departments Involved
To study improvement and construction of the new existing natural-gas transport corridor	SCO member countries	2004–2010	Oil and gas state-controlled companies of Uzbekistan, Tajik Ministry of Energy and Industry, and relevant departments of SCO member countries
Construction of natural gas pipelines through Kyrgyzstan and Kazakhstan from Turkmenistan, reaching Uzbekistan and ending at Xinjiang Province, China	SCO member countries	2004–2010	Natural gas transportation company of Uzbekistan, oil and gas state-controlled companies of Uzbekistan, Tajik Ministry of Energy and Industry, and relevant departments of SCO member countries
Studies on drawing up investment plans for the construction, transformation, and renewal of energy projects and the possibilities of solving financing issues	SCO member countries	2004–2010	State Energy Company of Uzbekistan, Tajik Ministry of Energy and Industry, Kyrgyzstan power companies, and relevant departments of SCO member countries
To explore unconventional renewable energy to obtain sources of electricity	SCO member countries	2004–2010	State Energy Company of Uzbekistan, Uzbek Academy of Sciences, Ministerial Meeting and Technology Center of Uzbekistan, Tajik Ministry of Energy and Industry, and relevant departments of SCO member countries
To take advantage of the contracting capability of SCO member countries to initiate reconstruction projects of Afghan hydropower stations	SCO member countries	Since 2004	State Energy Company of Uzbekistan, Tajik Ministry of Energy and Industry, and relevant departments of SCO member countries
To study the cooperation possibilities among SCO member countries in terms of jointly exploring and developing oil and gas fields	SCO member countries	Long-term	Oil and Gas Exploration and Development Company of Uzbekistan, oil and gas state-controlled companies of Uzbekistan, Tajik Ministry of Energy and Industry, and relevant departments of SCO member countries

Source: Info summarised from news and official website of SCO and PRC MFA.

Table 3: The History of FOCAC Conferences

Conference	Year	Paper Issued	Commitments
First Ministerial Conference	2000	Beijing Declaration of the FOCAC; Guideline of China-Africa Cooperation in Economic and Social Development	• Promote political cooperation, create a favourable environment for China-Africa business affiliation and trade; • Provide assistance to African countries; • Give preference to importing African products; • Establish China-Africa Joint Business Council and China-Africa Products Exhibition Centre to promote bilateral trade and to facilitate access for African products to the Chinese market; • Provide special funds to support well-established Chinese enterprises to invest in African countries; • Cancel RMB10 billion in HIPC and LDC debts; and • Send extra medical teams to African countries.
Second Ministerial Conference	2003	FOCAC—Addis Ababa Action Plan (2004–2006)	• Enhance cooperation in the development of human resources, train 10,000 African personnel; • Open up market and grant free tariff access for some commodities from the LDCs in Africa; • Strengthen their consultations on cooperation of natural resources exploration, particularly energy development, and work out modalities to promote the objectives; • Sponsor the 'Meeting in Beijing'; and • Increase people-to-people exchanges with Africa and hold a China-Africa Youth Festival.

Appendix

Conference	Year	Paper Issued	Commitments
Beijing Summit and Third Ministerial Conference	2006	Declaration of the Beijing Summit of the FOCAC; FOCAC—Beijing Action Plan (2007–2009)	• Double the 2006 assistance to Africa by 2009; • Provide US$3 billion of preferential loans and US$2 billion of preferential buyer's credits; • Set up CADF, the funding to reach US$5 billion to encourage Chinese companies to invest in African countries and support them; • Build an AU conference centre; • Cancel debts owed by HIPCs that matured at the end of 2005; • Increase the number of export items from 190 to over 440, offer zero-tariff treatment to the 30 African LDCs; • Establish three to five trade and economic cooperation zones; • Promote joint exploration and rational exploitation of energy and other resources through diversified forms of cooperation; • Help African countries turn their advantages in energy and resources into development strengths; • Step up scientific and technological cooperation in areas of common interest, including agricultural bio-technology, solar energy utilisation, geological survey, mining and development of new medicine; • Train 15,000 African professionals and send 100 senior agricultural experts to Africa. Set up 10 special agricultural centres; • Build 30 hospitals, provide artemisinin (anti-malaria drug) to the value of RMB300 million and build 30 malaria prevention and treatment centres in Africa; • Dispatch youth volunteers to Africa; and • Build 100 rural schools in Africa and increase Chinese scholarships for African students from 2,000 per year to 4,000 per year by 2009.

Conference	Year	Paper Issued	Commitments
Fourth Ministerial Conference	2009	Declaration of Sharm el-Sheikh of the FOCAC; FOCAC—Sharm el-Sheikh Action Plan (2010–2012)	• Establish a China-Africa partnership to respond to climate change and build 100 clean-energy projects for Africa; • Enhance cooperation with Africa in science and technology: launch a China-Africa science and technology partnership, carry out 100 joint scientific and technological research demonstration projects and accept 100 African postdoctoral fellows to conduct scientific research in China; • Provide US$10 billion concessional loans to African countries and set up a US$1 billion special loan for small and medium African businesses; • Cancel debts associated with interest-free government loans due to mature by the end of 2009; • Give zero-tariff treatment to 95% of products from African LDCs; • Increase Chinese-built agricultural technology demonstration centres in Africa to 20 and send 50 agricultural technology teams to Africa to train 2,000 African agricultural technicians; • Provide medical equipment and anti-malaria equipment worth RMB500 million to hospitals and malaria prevention and treatment centres, and train 3,000 doctors and nurses for Africa; • Build 50 China-Africa friendship schools, train 1,500 school principals and teachers, and increase Chinese scholarships to Africa to 5,500 by 2012; and • Launch a China-Africa joint research and exchange programme.

Appendix

Conference	Year	Paper Issued	Commitments
Fifth Ministerial Conference	2012	The Beijing Declaration of the Fifth Ministerial Conference of the FOCAC and the Beijing Action Plan (2013–2015)	• Tap its advantages in railway technology to support Africa's efforts in developing and modernising its railway networks; • Make active use of grants, interest-free loans and concessional loans to help the development of African countries; • Train 30,000 African professionals in various sectors, offer 18,000 government scholarships and take measures to improve the content and quality of the training programmes; • Launch the 'science and technology for a better life' campaign in Africa and implement the joint research and technology demonstration projects; • Prioritise infrastructure in China-Africa cooperation and strengthen cooperation in transport, telecommunications, radio and television, water conservancy, electricity, energy, and other areas of infrastructure development; • Support joint development and proper use of Africa's energy and resources by enterprises; • Help African countries translate their energy and resources strength into development strength; • Advance cooperation in clean energy and renewable resources projects in keeping with the principles of mutual benefit and sustainable development; • Offer US$20 billion of credit to African countries; and • Launch cooperation projects in science and technology, as well as information and communication technology, which will further help strengthen Africa's industrialisation processes.

Source: FOCAC Archives.

Table 4: Agreements and Achievements Related to Clean Energy Reached in EU-China Summits from 2001 to 2012

EU-China Summit	Achievement
The 3rd EU-China Summit	The two sides carried out extensive discussions on bilateral relations, the development of China and the EU and the regional and international issues of common concern and interest. The focus of the summit was China's entry into the WTO. Additionally, the two sides exchanged views on cooperation in the sectors of science and technology, energy, information, education, etc.
The 4th EU-China Summit	Leaders from both sides stressed the importance of dialogue in the trade sector and strengthening and expanding inter-departmental dialogues in the sectors of enterprise policies and regulations, information society, environment, energy, science and technology, satellite navigation, etc.
The 6th EU-China Summit	Leaders from both sides emphasised the significance of strengthening and expanding industry dialogues on a broad range of topics. The existing industry dialogues cover the important sectors of energy, environmental, regulatory, and industry policy; social information; 'digital Olympics' exchange; etc. This kind of cooperation is attracting widespread interest.
The 7th EU-China Summit	Leaders from the two sides both expressed satisfaction with the progress of cooperation in all the sectors. They also appreciated the new momentum of Energy Dialogues after the successful convening of the 5th EU-China Energy Conference. The Agreement on R&D Cooperation on the Peaceful Use of Nuclear Energy between the European Atomic Energy Community (Euratom) and the Government of the People's Republic of China was signed.
The 8th EU-China Summit	The two sides signed the Memorandum of Understanding of Strategic Dialogue in the Energy and Transportation Sectors between China and the EU. During the summit, both sides released the EU-China Joint Statement on Climate Change, which established the partnership between China and Europe in relation to climate change. It would strengthen the cooperation and dialogue in relation to climate change, including clean energy, and would promote sustainable development. It would also promote cooperation in the development, application and transfer of low-carbon technologies, such as advanced coal technology through carbon capture and storage to achieve 'zero emissions'. The two sides welcomed the signing of the Memorandum of Understanding as a start to China-EU strategic dialogue in the sectors of energy and transportation.

Appendix

EU-China Summit	Achievement
The 9th EU-China Summit	Leaders from the two sides welcomed the progress made in solidifying the partnership between China and the EU in relation to climate change. Both leaders appreciated the closer cooperation in the clean development mechanism advocated in Kyoto Protocol. They both attached great importance to significantly reducing the costs of key technology and its transfer, application, and promotion. Furthermore, full coordination and cooperation in relation to promotion of energy security, sustainable energy supply, innovation, and reduction of greenhouse gas emissions was emphasised. Additionally, they also emphasised the strategic significance of the China-EU High-Level Energy Working Group and regular China-EU Energy Cooperation Conferences, the strengthening cooperation on the Clean Coal Action Plan and energy efficiency, and the renewable energy action plan within the cooperation framework. China and the EU had a common concern in the need to ensure a reliable, economical, and sustainable energy supply. At the same time, both parties continued to emphasise cooperation in the sectors of energy and transportation.
The 10th EU-China Summit	Leaders from the two sides attached great importance to climate change issues and were willing to continue cooperation to jointly cope with the severe challenges brought by climate change. It was agreed that China and the EU would shoulder the 'common but differentiated responsibilities', rely on their respective capabilities and jointly be committed to stabilising the atmospheric concentrations of greenhouse gases, thereby preventing dangerous human interference with the climatic system. China and the EU agreed to take effective measures and advance mutually beneficial cooperation in the energy sector.
The 11th EU-China Summit	The two sides reached cooperative agreements, including the Joint Statement by the China-EU Clean Energy Centre (EC2), the China and EU Science and Technology Partnership Scheme and the China-EU Small and Medium-Sized Enterprises Cooperation Consensus. The leaders mainly discussed EU-China relations, the global economic and financial crisis, climate change and energy security, and exchanged views on issues of the Korean Peninsula and other regions. They stated their determination to strengthen cooperation and to undertake further work together to address the financial crisis, climate change, and other global challenges, and that they were actively committed to promoting coordination and cooperation in international affairs.

EU-China Summit	Achievement
The 12th EU-China Summit	The Chinese and EU leaders renewed the China and EU Science and Technology Cooperation Agreement, signed and started the Memorandum of Understanding of the Second Cooperation Phase of Near Zero Emissions of Carbon Project, signed the Memorandum of Cooperation Framework of Buildings' Efficiency and Quality, and the China-EU Finance Agreement of Environmental Governance Projects. The leaders agreed that the international community was facing severe challenges and needed a global response. Climate change, the financial crisis, energy and resources security, food security, the environment and public health security, and other global issues were emerging, and terrorism and other non-traditional security threats had become global concerns. It was agreed that the need for close cooperation and coordination in the international community to cope with global challenges was becoming increasingly urgent.
The 13th EU-China Summit	The leaders all agreed that it was necessary to take appropriate climate change and energy policies to support the joint efforts in energy conservation, improving energy efficiency, and promoting green low-carbon development efforts. They emphasised the further strengthening of the China and EU partnership on climate change and the policy dialogue and pragmatic cooperation under the framework of Energy Dialogue. The focus of cooperation should include renewable energy, energy efficiency, smart grid, and clean coal technology, including carbon capture and storage technology. Both sides agreed to encourage research units, especially small and medium-sized enterprises, to carry out energy cooperation in R&D to promote energy saving and emission reduction.
The 14th EU-China Summit	As an initiative from the 14th Summit in 2012, the first China-EU High-Level Meeting on Energy (HLME) was held in May 2012, between NEA, EC DG ENER, energy ministers of the then 27 EU Member States, and relevant ministers belonging to the NEC. NEA and EC DG ENER were in charge of organising the meeting, which was in a restricted and exclusive format. The China-EU Joint Declaration on Energy Security was signed in this meeting, and the China-EU strategic energy consumer partnership was announced.
The 15th EU-China Summit	The leaders redoubled their joint efforts to tackle global challenges, including sustainable development, environmental protection, climate change, and energy security. They also agreed to further deepen dialogue and cooperation on promoting low-carbon development under the EU-China Partnership on Climate Change.

Source: Info summarised from news and official website of European Commission and Chinese MFA.

Bibliography

ADB. 'ADB, AIIB Sign MOU to Strengthen Cooperation for Sustainable Growth'. ADB, 2016. https://www.adb.org/news/adb-aiib-sign-mou-strengthen-cooperation-sustainable-growth.

ADB. 'Meeting Asia's Infrastructure Needs'. ADB, 2017. https://www.adb.org/publications/asia-infrastructure-needs.

African Development Bank. 'African Economic Outlook 2020'. African Development Bank, 2020. https://www.afdb.org/sites/default/files/documents/publications/afdb20-04_aeo_supplement_full_report_for_web_0705.pdf.

African Natural Resources Center. 'Africa's Natural Resources Wealth: A Snap Shot'. African Natural Resources Center, 2015. http://www.afdb.org/en/topics-and-sectors/initiatives-partnerships/african-natural-resources-center-anrc/.

AIIB. 'AIIB Annual Report and Accounts 2016'. Asian Infrastructure Investment Bank, 2016. https://www.aiib.org/en/news-events/annual-report/2016/home/pdf/Annual_Report_2016.pdf.

AIIB. 'AIIB Annual Report and Accounts 2017'. Asian Infrastructure Investment Bank, 2017. https://www.aiib.org/en/news-events/annual-report/2017/_common/pdf/AIIB-Annual-Report-2017.pdf.

AIIB. 'Energy Sector Strategy: Sustainable Energy for Asia'. Asian Infrastructure Investment Bank, 2017. https://www.aiib.org/en/policies-strategies/strategies/sustainable-energy-asia/index.html.

Alessi, Christopher, and Beina Xu. 'China in Africa'. Council on Foreign Affairs, 2015. https://www.cfr.org/china/china-africa/p9557.

Alves, Ana Cristina. 'Chinese Economic Diplomacy in Africa: The Lusophone Strategy'. In *China Returns to Africa: A Rising Power and a Content Embrace*, edited by Chris Alden, Daniel Large, and Ricardo Soares de Oliveira, 69–82. Oxford: Oxford University Press, 2008.

Andrews-Speed, Philip. 'China's Energy Crisis: Unstoppable Force Meets Immoveable Object'. Philip Andrews-Speed personal page. http://www.andrewsspeed.com/chinas-energy-crisis-unstoppable-force-meets-immoveable-object/.

Andrews-Speed, Philip. *Energy Policy and Regulation in the People's Republic of China*, 355–366. London: Kluwer Law International, 2004.

Andrews-Speed, Philip. *The Strategic Implications of China's Energy Needs*. London: Routledge, 2014.

Asia Law. 'Risks for Chinese Investors in the One Belt One Road Initiative'. *Asialaw*, 2016. https://www.asialaw.com/articles/risks-for-chinese-investors-in-the-one-belt-one-road-initiative/armhdfdc.

Andrews-Speed, Philip, Stephen Dow, and Zhiguo Gao. 'A Provisional Evaluation of the 1998 Reforms to China's Government and State Sector: The Case of the Energy Industry'. *CEPMLP Journal* 4, no. 7 (1998): 1–11.

Bajpaee, Chietigj. 'China Fuels Energy Cold War'. *Asia Times*, 2 March 2005. http://www.atimes.com/atimes/China/GC02Ad07.html.

Baregu, Mwesiga. 'The Three Faces of the Dragon: Tanzania-China Relations in Historical Perspective'. In *Crouching Tiger, Hidden Dragon? Africa and China*, edited by Kweku Ampiah and Sanusha Naidu, 197–219. Scottsville: University of KwaZulu-Natal Press, 2008.

Barysch, Katinka, Charles Grant, and Mark Leonard. 'Embracing the Dragon: Can the EU and China Be Friends?' *CESifo Forum* 6, no. 3 (2005): 8–15.

BBC. 'China's Hu Boosts Kenyan Business'. *BBC*, 28 April 2006.

BBC. 'Guinea Elections: Alpha Condé Wins Third Term amid Violent Protests'. *BBC*, 24 October 2020. https://www.bbc.com/news/world-africa-54657359.

Bielecki, Janusz. 'Energy Security: Is the Wolf at the Door?' *The Quarterly Review of Economics and Finance* 42, no. 2 (2002): 235–250.

Blagov, Sergei. 'Russia Urges Formation of Central Asian Energy Club'. *Eurasianet*, 7 November 2007.

Blanchard, Jean-Marc. 'Harmonious World and China's Foreign Economic Policy: Features, Implications, and Challenges'. *Journal of Chinese Political Science* 13, no. 2 (2008): 165–192, 174.

Blank, Stephen. 'China, Kazakh Energy and Russia: An Unlikely Ménage à Trois'. *China and Eurasia Forum Quarterly* 3, no. 3 (2005): 99–109, 103;

Blank, Stephen. 'China's Defeats in Central Asia'. *Central Asia-Caucasus Analyst*, 14 August 2002.

Boo, Bee Chu. 'China Aims for Win-Win Partnership with African Mining Sector'. *Baker Mckenzie*, 2020. https://www.bakermckenzie.com/en/insight/publications/2020/01/china-partnership-with-african-mining-sector.

BP. *BP Statistical Review of World Energy (Gas) 2020*. London: BP, 2020.

BP. *BP Statistical Review of World Energy (Oil) 2020*. London: BP, 2020.

Breslin, Shaun. 'Power and Production: Rethinking China's Global Economic Role'. *Review of International Studies* 31, no. 4 (2005): 735–753.

Brummer, Matthew. 'The Shanghai Cooperation Organization and Iran: A Power-Full Union'. *Journal of International Affairs* 60, no. 2 (2007): 185–198, 185.

Calder, Kent. *Pacific Defense: Arms, Energy, and America's Future in Asia*. New York: William Morrow & Co., 2006.

Casaburi, Ivana. 'Chinese Investment in Europe'. ESADE China Europe Club, 2016. http://itemsweb.esade.edu/research/esadegeo/ENGChineseInvestmentInEurope201516.pdf.

CFR. 'China's Approach to Global Governance'. Council on Foreign Relations, 2021. https://www.cfr.org/china-global-governance/.

Chang, Felix K. 'Chinese Energy and Asian Security'. *Orbis* 145, no. 2 (2001): 211–240.

Chen, Shaofeng. 'Motivations behind China's Foreign Oil Quest: A Perspective from the Chinese Government and the Oil Companies'. *Journal of Chinese Political Science* 13, no. 1 (2008): 79–104.

Chen, Weidong, and Tom Cutler. 'The Outlook for a Chinese Pivot to Gas'. The National Bureau of Asian Research, 2014.

Chen, Wenjie, David Dollar, and Heiwai Tang. 'Why Is China Investing in Africa? Evidence from the Firm Level'. *World Bank Economic Review* 32, no. 3 (2018): 610–632.

Cherp, Aleh, Jessica Jewell, and Andrew Goldthau. 'Governing Global Energy: Systems, Transitions, Complexity'. *Global Policy* 2, no. 1 (2011): 75–88.
China Daily. 'China, Kazakhstan Discuss Cross-Border Gas Pipeline'. *China Daily*, 25 August 2004.
Christoffersen, Gaye. 'The Dilemmas of China's Energy Governance: Recentralization and Regional Cooperation'. *The China and Eurasia Form Quarterly* 3, no. 3 (2005): 55–80.
Christoffersen, Gaye. 'The Role of China in Global Energy Governance'. *China Perspectives* 1, no. 2 (2016): 15–24.
Clegg, Jeremy, and Hinrich Voss. 'Chinese Overseas Direct Investment in the European Union'. In *China and the EU in Context*, edited by Kerry Brown, 14–43. London: Palgrave Macmillan, 2014.
Clowes, William. 'China Marks Cobalt, Copper Ascendancy in Congo with New Group'. *Bloomberg*, 18 June 2018. https://www.bloomberg.com/news/articles/2018-06-18/china-marks-cobalt-copper-ascendancy-in-congo-with-new-group.
CNPC, 'CNPC in Kazakhstan'. CNPC, 2008.
CNPC. 'Central Asia-China Gas Pipeline'. CNPC, 2010. https://www.cnpc.com.cn/en/CentralAsia/CentralAsia_index.shtml.
CNPC. 'CNPC in Kazakhstan'. Accessed 3 March 2012. http://classic.cnpc.com.cn/en/cnpcworldwide/kazakhstan.
CNPC. 'Flow of natural gas from Central Asia'. CNPC, 2013. http://www.cnpc.com.cn/en/FlowofnaturalgasfromCentralAsia/FlowofnaturalgasfromCentralAsia2.shtml.
Constantin, Christian. 'China's Conception of Energy Security: Sources and International Impacts'. Working Paper no. 43, The University of British Columbia, 2005. https://sppga.ubc.ca/news/chinas-conception-of-energy-security-sources-and-international-impacts/.
CPCIF. *China Petroleum and Chemical Industry Federation Annual Report 2010*. Beijing: CPCIF, 2011.
Crane, Keith. *Imported Oil and US National Security*. Washington: RAND Corporation, 2009.
Dahir, Abdi Latif. 'Twice as Many African Presidents Made It to China's Africa Summit Than to the UN General Assembly'. *Quartz Africa*, 5 October 2018.
De Matteis, Pietro. 'EU-China Cooperation in the Field of Energy, Environment and Climate Change'. *Journal of Contemporary European Research* 6, no. 4 (2010): 449–477.
Delegation of the European Union to China. 2012. 'Inauguration of China-EU Institute for Clean and Renewable Energy at Huazhong University of Science and Technology'. http://eeas.europa.eu/delegations/china/press_corner/all_news/news/2012/20121030_en.htm.
Dollar, David. 'China as a Global Investor'. Working Paper 4, Brookings Institute, 2016.
Downs, Erica. 'Brookings Foreign Studies Energy Security Series: China'. Brookings, 2006. https://www.brookings.edu/research/brookings-foreign-policy-studies-energy-security-series-china/.
Downs, Erica. 'Mission Mostly Accomplished: China's Energy Trade and Investment along the Silk Road Economic Belt'. *China Brief* 15, no. 6 (2015): 3–6.
Dubash, Navroz K., and Ann Florini. 'Mapping Global Energy Governance'. *Global Policy* 2, no. 1 (2011): 6–18.
Dwivedi, Ramakant. 'China's Central Asia Policy in Recent Times'. *China and Eurasia Forum Quarterly* 4, no. 4 (2006): 145–157.
E3G. 'China's New NDC – E3G Responds'. E3G, 2022. https://www.e3g.org/news/china-s-new-ndc-e3g-responds/.
EC2. 'Know More about EC2'. EC2, 2014. http://www.ec2.org.cn/.

Economist. 'Why China Is Creating a New "World Bank" for Asia'. *Economist*, 11 November 2014. https://www.economist.com/blogs/economist-explains/2014/11/economist-explains-6.
Edinger, Hannah. 'Colonial Ambitions?' *New Matilda*, 2008. https://newmatilda.com/2008/08/11/colonial-ambitions.
EID. 'Chinese Oil Firms "Go Out" to Resolve the Oil Predicament'. *Economic Information Daily*, 21 September 2004. http://finance.sina.com.cn/g/20040921/08431037218.shtml.
Energy Charter. 'The International Energy Charter'. Energy Charter, 2015. https://www.energycharter.org/process/international-energy-charter-2015/overview/.
Energy Intelligence. 'Major Target: Chinese Set Their Sights on Kazakhstan'. *Energy Intelligence*, 21 July 2003. https://www.energyintel.com/0000017b-a7a1-de4c-a17b-e7e331280001.
Energy Research Institute and Grantham Institute. *Global Energy Governance Reform and China's Participation: Consultation Draft Report*. London: Grantham Institute, 2014.
Ericsson, Magnus, Olof Löf, and Anton Löf. 'Chinese Control over African and Global Mining—Past, Present and Future'. *Mineral Economics* 33, no. 1 (2020): 153–181.
Escobar, Pepe. 'The Eurasian Big Bang: How China and Russia Are Carving Out Their Own World Order'. *Energy Post*, 25 August 2015.
European Commission. 'A 2030 Framework for Climate and Energy Policies'. European Commission, 2021. https://ec.europa.eu/clima/eu-action/climate-strategies-targets/2030-climate-energy-framework_en.
European Commission. 'A European Strategy for Sustainable, Competitive and Secure Energy'. European Commission, 2006. https://eur-lex.europa.eu/EN/legal-content/summary/green-paper-a-european-strategy-for-sustainable-competitive-and-secure-energy.html.
European Commission. 'A Long Term Policy for China-Europe Relations'. European Commission, 1995. https://op.europa.eu/en/publication-detail/-/publication/0bcbc1c7-2c78-4bba-a027-f67035eeac4f.
European Commission. 'Building a Comprehensive Partnership with China'. European Commission, 1998. https://eur-lex.europa.eu/LexUriServ/LexUriServ.do?uri=COM:1998:0181:FIN:EN:PDF.
European Commission. 'Communication from the Commission—Energy for the Future: Renewable Sources of Energy—White Paper for a Community Strategy and Action Plan'. European Commission, 1997.
European Commission. 'Critical Raw Materials Resilience: Charting a Path towards Greater Security and Sustainability'. European Commission, 2020. https://eur-lex.europa.eu/legal-content/EN/TXT/HTML/?uri=CELEX:52020DC0474&from=EN.
European Commission. 'Energy from Abroad'. European Commission, 2014. http://ec.europa.eu/energy/international/bilateral_cooperation/china/china_en.htm.
European Commission. 'EU-China 2020 Strategic Agenda for Cooperation'. European Commission, 2013. https://www.eeas.europa.eu/sites/default/files/20131123.pdf.
European Commission. 'EU-China Cooperation on Energy Issues'. European Commission, 2021. https://energy.ec.europa.eu/topics/international-cooperation/key-partner-countries-and-regions/china_en#the-annual-energy-dialogue.
European Commission. 'EU-China Energy Working Group Approved'. European Commission, 1996. http://europa.eu/rapid/press-release_IP-96-1242_en.htm.
European Commission. 'EU-China Roadmap on Energy Cooperation (2016–2020)'. European Commission, 2016. https://ec.europa.eu/energy/sites/ener/files/documents/FINAL_EU_CHINA_ENERGY_ROADMAP_EN.pdf.

European Commission. 'European Commission and HR/VP Contribution to the European Council: EU-China—A Strategic Outlook'. European Commission, 2019. https://ec.europa.eu/info/sites/default/files/communication-eu-china-a-strategic-outlook.pdf.

European Commission. 'European Union, Trade with China'. European Commission, 2021. https://webgate.ec.europa.eu/isdb_results/factsheets/country/details_china_en.pdf.

European Commission. 'Questions and Answers on the Communication on Demonstrating Carbon Capture and Geological Storage (CCS) in Emerging Developing Countries: Financing the EU-China Near Zero Emissions Coal Plant Project'. European Commission, 2009. https://ec.europa.eu/commission/presscorner/detail/es/MEMO_09_295.

European Commission. 'The Agreement between the People's Republic of China and the European Community'. European Commission, 1978. http://aei.pitt.edu/8243/1/31735055282234_1.pdf.

European Parliament, 'Making solar a source of EU energy security', European Parliament, 2022, https://www.europarl.europa.eu/RegData/etudes/ATAG/2022/733587/EPRS_ATA(2022)733587_EN.pdf.

Fan, Bi. *The New World Energy Order: The Impact of US 'Energy Independence' and China's Response*. Beijing: China Economy Publisher, 2014.

Feng, G. *Annual Report on China's Outbound Direct Investment and Host Country Risks*. Beijing: Social Sciences Academic Press, 2017.

Florini, Ann, and Benjamin Sovacool. 'Bridging the Gaps in Global Energy Governance'. *Global Governance* 17, no. 1 (2011): 57–74.

Florini, Ann. 'The International Energy Agency in Global Energy Governance'. *Global Policy* 2, no. 1 (2011): 40–50.

FOCAC. 'China Looking for Redoubled Cooperation with Africa'. FOCAC Archives, 2006. http://www.focac.org/eng/zt/zgdfzzcwj/t231169.htm.

FOCAC. 'Forum on China-Africa Cooperation Beijing Action Plan (2007–2009)'. FOCAC Archives. http://www.focac.org/eng/ltda/dscbzjhy/DOC32009/t280369.htm.

FOCAC. 'Forum on China-Africa Cooperation Sharm El Sheikh Action Plan (2010–2012)'. FOCAC Archives, 2009. http://www.focac.org/eng/ltda/dsjbzjhy/hywj/t626387.htm.

FOCAC. 'Forum on China-Africa Cooperation: Addis Ababa Action Plan'. FOCAC Archives, 2004. http://www.focac.org/eng/ltda/dejbzjhy/DOC22009/.

FOCAC. 'Programme for China-Africa Cooperation in Economic and Social Development'. FOCAC Archives, 2009. http://www.focac.org/eng/ltda/dyjbzjhy/DOC12009/t606797.htm.

FOCAC. 'The Fifth Ministerial Conference of the Forum on China-Africa Cooperation Beijing Action Plan (2013–2015)'. FOCAC Archives, 2012. http://www.focac.org/eng/ltda/dwjbzjjhys/hywj/t954620.htm.

FOCAC. 'To Achieve Common Development and Prosperity Through Joint Efforts of China and Africa'. FOCAC Archives, 2012. http://www.focac.org/eng/ltda/t967201.htm.

Forbes. 'Turkmenistan to Join China, Kazakhstan Pipeline Project—KazMunaiGas EP CEO'. *Forbes AFX News*, 4 July 2007.

Friedman, Edward. 'China-Driven Development as China Pours Billions into Africa, Other Countries Are Trying to Keep Up'. *Beijing Review*, 1 February 2009. http://www.bjreview.com/world/txt/2009-02/01/content_176304.htm.

Garrison, Jean. *China and the Energy Equation in Asia: The Determinants of Policy Choice*. Boulder, CO: Lynne Rienner Publishers, 2009.

Ghosh, Arunabha. 'Seeking Coherence in Complexity? The Governance of Energy by Trade and Investment Institutions'. *Global Policy* 2, no. 1 (2011): 106–119.

Ghoshray, Atanu, and Javier Ordóñez, 'The Chinese Energy-Intensive Growth Model and Its Impact on Commodity Markets'. In *Energy Security and Sustainable Economic Growth in China*, edited by Shujie Yao and Maria Jesus Herrerias Herrerias, 31-51. London: Palgrave Macmillan, 2014.

Glaser, Bonnie. 'China's Grand Strategy in Asia'. CSIS, 2014. https://csis-website-prod.s3.amazonaws.com/s3fs-public/legacy_files/files/attachments/ts140313_glaser.pdf.

Global Times. 'China Searches for Solution after Being Hit by Natural Gas Shortage'. *Global Times*, 1 January 2018. http://www.globaltimes.cn/content/1083117.shtml.

Goldthau, Andreas, and Jan Martin Witte. 'Back to the Future or Forward to the Past? Strengthening Markets and Rules for Effective Global Energy Governance'. *International Affairs* 85, no. 2 (2009): 373–390.

Goldthau, Andreas, and Jan Martin Witte. *Global Energy Governance: The New Rules of the Game*, 99–104. Washington, DC: Brookings Press, 2010.

Goldthau, Andreas. 'Governing Global Energy: Existing Approaches and Discourses'. *Current Opinion in Environmental Sustainability* 3, no. 4 (2011): 213–217.

Goldthau, Andreas. 'The Public Policy Dimension of Energy Security'. In *The Routledge Handbook of Energy Security*, edited by Benjamin Sovacool, 129–145. London: Routledge, 2011.

Golovnina, Maria. 'Kazakhstan, China Agree on Pipeline from Caspian'. *Reuters*, 18 August 2007.

Grenville, Stephen. 'The Asian Infrastructure Investment Bank and the Rise of Regionalism'. Lowy Institute, 2015. https://www.lowyinstitute.org/the-interpreter/asian-infrastructure-investment-bank-and-rise-regionalism.

Grevi, Giovanni, and Vasconcelos Alvaro. 'Partnerships for Effective Multilateralism: EU Relations with Brazil, China, India and Russia'. *Chaillot Paper* 109, 2008. http://www.iss.europa.eu/publications/detail/article/partnerships-for-effective-multilateralism-eu-relations-with-brazil-china-india-and-russia/.

Gross, Samantha. 'Global China: Global Governance and Norms'. Brookings Institute, 2021. https://www.brookings.edu/research/global-china-global-governance-and-norms/.

Guo, Shizhi. 'The Business Development of China's National Oil Companies: The Government to Business Relationship in China'. Working Paper, Rice University, 2007.

Hall, Peter. 'Policy Paradigms, Social Learning and the State: The Case of Economic Policymaking in Britain'. *Comparative Politics* 25 (1993): 275–297.

Handke, Susann. 'Securing and Fuelling China's Ascent to Power: The Geopolitics of the Chinese-Kazakh Oil Pipeline'. Working Paper, Clingendael Institute of International Relations, 2006.

Haugwitz, Frank. 'EU-China Energy and Environment Program'. Presentation Paper, Conference of Wind Power Shanghai, 2007. http://www.frankhaugwitz.info/doks/aboutme/2007_11_02_EEP_RE_Shanghai_Wind_Power_Conference.pdf.

Hay, Colin. 'The "Crisis" of Keynesianism and the Rise of Neoliberalism in Britain: An Ideational Institutionalist Approach'. In *The Rise of Neoliberalism and Institutional Analysis*, edited by John L. Campbell and Ove K. Pedersen, 193–218. Princeton, NJ: Princeton University Press, 2001.

Bibliography

Helm, Dieter. 'The New Energy Paradigm'. In *The New Energy Paradigm*, edited by Dieter Helm, 9–35. Oxford: Oxford University Press, 2007.

Heppell, Janice K. M. 'Confidence-Building Measures: Bilateral versus Multilateral Approaches'. In *Peace and Security in Northeast Asia: The Nuclear Issue and the Korean Peninsula*, edited by Yong Whan Kihl and Peter Hayers, 269–304. London: Routledge, 1997.

Higgott, Richard. 'Multilateralism and the Limits of Global Governance'. Working Paper No. 134/04, CSGR, 2004.

Hook, Leslie. 'Kazakhstan Embraces Chinese Investment'. *Financial Times*, 22 February 2011.

Hornby, Lucy. 'China Seeks Foreign Investors for One Belt, One Road Push'. *Financial Times*, 25 May 2016.

ICARE. 'The ICARE Institute'. Institute for Clean and Renewable Energy, 2013. http://www.ce-icare.eu/en/article/26/26-en-the-icare-institute.

IEA. 'Africa Faces Both Major Challenges and Huge Opportunities as It Transitions to Clean Energy'. IEA, 2022. https://www.iea.org/news/africa-faces-both-major-challenges-and-huge-opportunities-as-it-transitions-to-clean-energy.

IEA. 'Boosting the Power Sector in Sub-Saharan Africa: China's Involvement: International Energy Agency'. IEA, 2016. https://www.iea.org/publications/freepublications/publication/Partner_Country_SeriesChinaBoosting_the_Power_Sector_in_SubSaharan_Africa_Chinas_Involvement.pdf.

IEA. 'China's Engagement in Global Energy Governance'. OECD, 2015. https://www.oecd.org/publications/china-s-engagement-in-global-energy-governance-9789264255845-en.htm.

IEA. 'World Energy Outlook 2021'. IEA, 2021. https://www.iea.org/reports/world-energy-outlook-2021.

IEA. *China's Worldwide Quest for Energy Security*. Paris: IEA, 2000.

IEA. *World Energy Outlook 2007: China and India Insights*. Paris: OECD, 2007.

Ikenberry, John. 'The Rise of China and the Future of the West: Can the Liberal System Survive?' *Foreign Affairs* 87, no. 1 (2008): 23–37.

Jaffe, Amy Myers, and Steven Lewis. 'Beijing's Oil Diplomacy'. *Survival* 44, no. 1 (2002): 115–134.

Jakobson, Linda, and Dean Knox. 'New Foreign Policy Actors in China'. SIPRI Policy Paper No. 26, Peace Research Institute, 2010. https://www.files.ethz.ch/isn/120962/SIPRIPP26.pdf.

Keohane, Robert. 'Multilateralism: An Agenda for Research'. *Canada's Journal of Global Policy Analysis* 45, no. 4 (1990): 731.

Kerr, David, and Laura C. Swinton. 'China, Xinjiang and the Transnational Security of Central Asia'. *Critical Asian Studies* 40, no. 1 (2008): 89–112.

Kerr, David, and Yanzhou Xu. 'Europe, China, and Security Governance: Is There Evidence of Normative Convergence?' *Asia Europe Journal* 12, no. 1–2 (2012): 79–93.

Khan, Hamayoun. 'China's Energy Drive and Diplomacy'. *International Review* (2008): 91–108.

Kimmage, Daniel. 'Central Asia: Turkmenistan-China Pipeline Project Has Far-Reaching Implications'. *Radio Free Europe/Radio Liberty*, 10 April 2006.

Knodt, Michele, and Nadine Piefer. *Challenges of European External Energy Governance with Emerging Powers*. Surrey: Ashgate, 2015.

Koh, Gui Qing. 'How China Decided to Redraw the Global Financial Map'. *Reuters*, 17 September 2015.

Kong, Bo. 'An Anatomy of China's Energy Insecurity and Its Strategies'. Pacific Northwest Laboratory for the United States Department of Energy, 2005. https://www.pnnl.gov/main/publications/external/technical_reports/pnnl-15529.pdf.
Kong, Bo. 'Governing China's Energy in the Context of Global Governance'. *Global Policy* 2, no. 1 (2011): 51–65.
Kong, Bo. 'Institutional insecurity'. *China Security* 3 (2006): 64–88.
Krueger, Robert B. *The United States and International Oil*. New York: Praeger Publisher, 1975.
Kynge, James. 'Western Resistance to China Blocks $40bn of Acquisitions'. *Financial Times*, 25 October 2016.
Langenkamp, Dobie. 'Our Friend, The Dragon'. *Energy Tribune*, 2010. http://www.energytribune.com/articles.cfm?aid=3758.
Lanteigne, Marc. 'China's Maritime Security and the "Malacca Dilemma"'. *Asian Security* 4, no. 2 (2008): 143–161.
Lanteigne, Marc. *China and International Institutions: Alternate Paths to Global Power*. London: Routledge, 2005.
Ledesma, David. 'East Africa Gas—Potential for Export'. Report, Oxford Institute for Energy Studies, 2013.
Lee, Henry, Daniel Schrag, Matthew Bunn, Michael Davidson, Wei Peng, Wang Pu, and Mao Zhimin. *Foundations for a Low-Carbon Energy System in China*. Cambridge: Cambridge University Press, 2021.
Legault, G.-F. 'AIIB Melding, Not Moulding Global Governance'. East Asia Forum, 2015. http://www.eastasiaforum.org/2015/11/18/aiib-melding-not-moulding-global-governance.
Lema, Rasmus. 'China's Investments in Renewable Energy in Africa: Creating Co-benefits or Just Cashing-In?' *World Development* 141 (2021): 1–18.
Leung, Guy. 'China's Energy Security: Perception and Reality'. *Energy Policy* 39, no. 3 (2011): 1330–1337.
Lewis, Jeff, and Melanie Burton. 'Chinese Miners' Deal Frenzy Seen Stalling on Regulatory Hurdles'. *Reuters*, 6 July 2020.
Li, Cunhui. '中哈原油管道合作双赢开辟能源通道' [Win-win situation in Sino-Kazakhstan oil pipeline open energy corridor]. *China Petroleum Daily*, 17 December 2010.
Li, Zhaoxing. 'Peace, Development and Cooperation—Banner for China's Diplomacy in the New Era'. *Chinese Journal of International Law* 4, no. 2 (2005): 677–683.
Lieberthal, Kenneth, and Michel Oksenberg. *Policy Making in China: Leaders, Structures and Process*. Princeton, NJ: Princeton University Press, 1988.
Lim, Robyn. *Geopolitics of East Asia: The Search for Equilibrium*. New York: Routledge, 2005.
Lin, Kun-Chin. 'Disembedding Socialist Firms as a Statist Project: Restructuring the Chinese Oil Industry, 1997–2002'. *Enterprise & Society* 7, no. 1 (2006): 59–97.
Liou, Chih-shian. 'Bureaucratic Politics and Overseas Investment by Chinese State-Owned Oil Companies: Illusory Champions'. *Asian Survey* 49, no. 4 (2009): 670–690.
Lu, Ting'en. 'The Example of Summit Diplomacy between China and African Premier Zhou Enlai's First Visit to Africa'. In *China and Africa*, edited by Center for African Studies, Peking University. Beijing: Peking University Press, 2005.
Magnus, George. 'China Must Prove Silk Road Plan Is Serious'. *Financial Times*. 4 May 2015.
Maltby, Tomas. 'European Union Energy Policy Integration: A Case of European Commission Policy Entrepreneurship and Increasing Supranationalism'. *Energy Policy* 55 (2013): 435–444.
Mearsheimer, John. 'China's Unpeaceful Rise'. *Current History* 105, no. 690 (2006): 160–162.

Meidan, Michal, Philip Andrews-Speed, and Ma Xin, 'Shaping China's Energy Policy: Actors and Processes'. *Journal of Contemporary China* 18, no. 61 (2009): 591–616.

Miles, Kahler. 'Multilateralism with Small and Large Numbers'. *International Organization* 46, no. 3 (1992): 681.

Moran, Theodore H. *China's Strategy to Secure Natural Resources: Risks, Dangers, and Opportunities*. Washington: Peterson Institute for International Economics, 2010.

Morse, Julia, and Robert Keohane. 'Contested Multilateralism'. *Review of International Organizations* 9, no. 4 (2014): 385–412.

Mufson, Steven. 'As China, U.S. Vie for More Oil, Diplomatic Friction May Follow'. *Washington Post*, 15 April 2006. http://www.washingtonpost.com/wp-dyn/content/article/2006/04/14/AR2006041401682_2.html.

Munro, Ross H. 'China's Relations with Its Neighbours'. *International Journal* 61, no. 2 (2006): 320–328, 327.

Naughton, Barry. 'SASAC and Rising Corporate Power in China'. *China Leadership Monitor* 24 (2008): 1–9.

Nurshayeva, Raushan, and Shamil Zhumatov. 'China's Hu Boosts Energy Ties with Central Asia'. *Reuters*, 12 December 2009.

O'Sullivan, Meghan. *Windfall: How the new energy abundance upends global politics and strengthens America's power*. New York: Simon & Schuster, 2017.

Ofosu, George, and David Sarpong. 'China in Africa: On the Competing Perspectives of the Value of Sino-Africa Business Relationships'. *Journal of Economic* 56, no. 1 (2022): 137–157.

OGJ. 'CNPC Completes Buy of Stake off Mozambique'. *Oil & Gas Journal*, 23 July 2013. http://www.ogj.com/articles/2013/07/cnpc-completes-buy-of-stake-off-mozambique.html.

OGJ. 'Russian-Chinese Competition May Marginalize US, European Influence'. *Oil and Gas Journal*, 13 March 2006. http://www.ogj.com/articles/print/volume-104/issue-10/exploration-development/central-asia-oil-and-gas-2-russian-chinese-competition-may-marginalize-us-european-influence.html.

Oxfam. 'The AIIB's Energy Opportunity: How the Asian Infrastructure Investment Bank's Energy Lending Can Chart a New Path of Sustainable Development'. Oxfam, 2017. https://www.oxfam.org/sites/www.oxfam.org/files/file_attachments/bn-the-aiibs-energy-opportunity-150617-en.pdf.

Paik, Keunwook, Marcel Valerie, Lahn Glada, and John V. Mitchell, and Erkin Adylov. 'Trends in Asian National Oil Company Investments Abroad: An Update'. Working Paper, Chatham House, 2007. http://www.chathamhouse.org.uk/files/6427_r0307anoc.pdf.

Paik, Keunwook. 'Sino-Russian Gas and Oil Cooperation: Entering into a New Era of Strategic Partnership?'. Oxford Institute for Energy Studies, 2015. https://www.oxfordenergy.org/wpcms/wp-content/uploads/2015/04/WPM-59.pdf.

Parameswaran, Prashanth. 'The Real Trouble with China's Belt and Road'. *The Diplomat*, 11 May 2017. https://thediplomat.com/2017/05/the-real-trouble-with-chinas-belt-and-road/.

Paramonov, Vladimir. 'China and Central Asia: Present and Future of Economic Relations'. Working Paper, Conflict Studies Research Centre, 2005.

Pavlićević, Dragan. 'China, the EU and One Belt, One Road strategy'. *China Brief* 15, no. 15 (2015). http://www.jamestown.org/programs/chinabrief/single/?tx_ttnews%5Btt_news%5D=44235&cHash=9dbc08472c19ecd691307c4c1905eb0c#.V9-58CTuCXs.

People's Daily. 'Good Friends, Good Partners and Good Brothers'. *People's Daily Online*, 22 June 2006. http://en.people.cn/200606/22/eng20060622_276333.html.

People's Daily. 'Kazakhstan–China Oil Pipeline to Open in May'. *People's Daily Online*, 27 February 2006.
People's Daily. 'Premier Li Peng Put Forward Six Proposals on Economic and Trade Cooperation between China and Central Asian Countries'. *People's Daily*, 27 April 1994.
People's Daily. '中、塔、俄、哈、吉五国《杜尚别声明》' [Tajikistan, Russia, Kazakhstan, and Kyrgyz signed the Dushanbe Declaration]. *People's Daily*, 5 July 2000.
Peyrouse, Sébastien. 'Central Asia's Growing Partnership with China'. Working Paper, EUCAM, 2008.
Peyrouse, Sébastien. 'Economic Aspects of the Chinese–Central Asia Rapprochement'. Working Paper, Central Asia–Caucasus Institute & Silk Road Studies Program, 2007.
Pop, Irina Ionela. 'China's Energy Strategy in Central Asia: Interactions with Russia, India and Japan'. *UNISCI Discussion Papers* 24 (2010): 197–220.
Pottinger, Matt. 'CNOOC Drops Offer for Unocal, Exposing U.S.-Chinese Tensions'. *Wall Street Journal*, 3 August 2005. https://www.wsj.com/articles/SB112295744495102393.
PRC MEE. 'China-Africa Declaration on Climate Change'. PRC MEE, 2021. https://www.mee.gov.cn/ywdt/hjywnews/202112/t20211202_962652.shtml.
PRC MFA. 'Bilateral Relationship between China and Turkmenistan'. PRC MFA, 2007. http://www.mfa.gov.cn/chn/wjb/zzjg/dozys/gjlb/1781/default.htm.
PRC MFA. 'China and African Countries Celebrate the 50th Anniversary of Diplomatic Relations'. PRC MFA, 2006. http://www.fmprc.gov.cn/ce/cebw/eng/xnyfgk/t257854.htm.
PRC MFA. 'China's Diplomacy in 2021: Embracing a Global Vision and Serving the Nation and Its People'. PRC MFA, 2021. https://www.fmprc.gov.cn/mfa_eng/wjb_663304/wjbz_663308/2461_663310/202112/t20211220_10471930.html.
PRC MFA. 'China-EU Scientific and Technological Cooperation and Exchange'. PRC MFA, 2004. http://www.fmprc.gov.cn/ce/cebe/eng/kj/t72211.htm.
PRC MFA. 'Chinese Government Issues African Policy Paper'. PRC MFA, 2006. https://www.mfa.gov.cn/ce/cegh//eng/xwdt/t231007.htm.
PRC MFA. 'Dushanbe Declaration of Heads of SCO Member States'. PRC MFA, 2008. https://www.mfa.gov.cn/ce/cgsf//eng/xw/t513027.htm.
PRC MFA. 'FOCAC Ministerial Meetings and Beijing Summits'. PRC MFA, 2012. https://www.mfa.gov.cn/ce/cemg//chn/zt/zfhzlt/t982253.htm.
PRC MFA. 'Follow-Up of the Fourth FOCAC Ministerial Meeting'. PRC MFA, 2012. https://www.mfa.gov.cn/ce/cerw//chn/rdzt/t952918.htm.
PRC MFA. 'Joint Communique of Meeting of Council of Heads of SCO Members'. PRC MFA, 2013. http://www.fmprc.gov.cn/mfa_eng/wjdt_665385/2649_665393/t355665.shtml.
PRC MFA. 'SCO Prime Ministers Discuss Cooperation in Astana'. PRC MFA, 2008. http://www.china-embassy.org/eng/ywzn/lsyw/oca/200810/t20081030_4904545.htm.
PRC MFA. 'The Eighth SCO Prime Ministers' Meeting Is Held in Beijing Wen Jiabao Chairs the Meeting'. PRC MFA, 2009. https://www.mfa.gov.cn/ce/cgsf//eng/xw/t620813.htm.
PRC MFA. 'Vice Minister of Commerce Wei Jianguo: China-Africa Economic and Trade Cooperation with Impressive Results'. PRC MFA, 2006. http://www.gov.cn/zwhd/2006-01/13/content_157162.htm.
PRC MFA. '上海合作组织成员国总理会议' [Shanghai Cooperation Organization (SCO) meeting]. PRC MFA, 2013. http://www.fmprc.gov.cn/mfa_chn/wjb_602314/zzjg_602420/dozys_602828/dqzzoys_602832/shhz_602834_1/gk_602836.
PRC MFA. *China's Diplomacy (2007)*. Beijing: World Affairs Press, 2007.

PRC MFA. *China's Diplomacy (2008)*. Beijing: World Affairs Press, 2008.
PRC MLR. 'The Main Functions'. PRC MLR, 2010. http://www.mlr.gov.cn/bbgk/zyzn/201009/t20100908_762243.htm.
PRC MOFCOM. 'Country Guide for Foreign Investment and Cooperation: Sudan (2021)'. PRC MOFCOM, 2021. http://www.mofcom.gov.cn/dl/gbdqzn/upload/sudan.pdf.
PRC MOST. '国际科技合作实施纲要' [Outline for Implementation of International Science and Technology Cooperation]. PRC MOST, 2006.
PRC MOST. '第八次中欧能源合作大会在上海召开' [The Eighth EU-China Energy Cooperation Conference held in Shanghai]'. PRC MOST, 2010, http://losangeles.china-consulate.org/chn/jbwzlm/ywzn/tech/news/201007/t20100727_5420927.htm.
PRC NBS. *China Energy Statistical Yearbook 2013*. Beijing: China Statistics Press, 2013.
PRC NDRC, PRC MFA, and PRC MOFCOM. 'Vision and Actions on Jointly Building the Silk Road Economic Belt and the 21st-Century Maritime Silk Road'. PRC NDRC, 2015. https://www.fmprc.gov.cn/eng/topics_665678/2015zt/xjpcxbayzlt2015nnh/201503/t20150328_705553.html.
PRC NDRC. 'Action Plan for Carbon Dioxide China'. PRC NDRC, 2021. https://en.ndrc.gov.cn/policies/202110/t20211027_1301020.html.
PRC NDRC. 'China's Energy Conditions and Policies', 2007. https://en.ndrc.gov.cn/policies/202105/P020210527780237298276.pdf.
PRC NDRC. '能源发展"十一五"规划' [Energy development 'Eleventh Five-Year' Plan], 2007. http://zfxxgk.nea.gov.cn/auto79/201109/P020110921527315023013.pdf.
PRC NEA. 'Cooperation between China and EU Countries in the Field of Energy'. PRC NEA, 2020. https://obor.nea.gov.cn/pictureDetails.html?id=2751.
PRC NEA. 'More Opportunities for Green Cooperation as China, Europe Lead Fight against Climate Change'. PRC NEA, 2020.
PRC NEA. 'Vision and Actions on Energy Cooperation in Jointly Building Silk Road Economic Belt and 21st-Century Maritime Silk Road'. PRC NDRC, 2017. http://www.nea.gov.cn/2017-05/12/c_136277478.htm.
PRC NEA. 'Wang Yi on the Four Aspects of Developing China-Europe Union (EU) Relations'. PRC NEA, 2020. https://obor.nea.gov.cn/detail2/14023.html.
PRC NEA. '第六次中欧能源对话在京举行' [The Sixth China-EU Energy Dialogue was held in Beijing]. PRC NEA, 2013. http://www.nea.gov.cn/2013-11/27/c_132923326.htm.
PRC NEA. 《2009年能源经济形势及2010年展望》 [2009 Energy Economic Situation and Prospects 2010]. Beijing: NEA, 2010.
PRC NPC. 'Renewable Energy Law of the People's Republic of China'. PRC NPC, 2005. http://www.npc.gov.cn/zgrdw/englishnpc/Law/2007-12/13/content_1384096.htm.
PRC SASAC. '中化集团与哈萨克磷公司签署战略合作框架协议' [Sinochem signed framework agreement with KPC]. PRC SASAC, 2011. http://www.sasac.gov.cn/n86114/n326638/c958714/content.html.
PRC SCOI. 'China's Foreign Aid'. PRC SCOI, 2011. http://www.scio.gov.cn/zxbd/nd/2011/Document/896869/896869.htm.
PRC SETC. 中国工业五十年: 1949–999 [Fifty years of China's industry]. Beijing: China Economy Publishing, 2000.
PRC State Council. 'An Overview of "Going Out" Strategy'. PRC State Council, 2011. http://qwgzyj.gqb.gov.cn/yjytt/159/1743.shtml.
PRC State Council. 'An Overview of China Renewable Energy Twelfth Five Year Plan'. PRC State Council, 2013. http://www.gov.cn/zwgk/2013-01/23/content_2318554.htm.

PRC State Council. 'China Trade Cooperation with Africa'. PRC State Council, 2010. http://www.gov.cn/zwgk/2010-12/23/content_1771638.htm.
PRC State Council. 'Government Issues African Policy Paper'. PRC State Council, 2006. http://www.gov.cn/misc/2006-01/12/content_156509.htm.
PRC State Council. 'The 11th Five-Year Plan for Economic and Social Development of the People's Republic of China (2006–2010)'. PRC State Council, 2006. http://www.gov.cn/gongbao/content/2006/content_268766.htm.
PRC State Council. 'The 11th Five-Year Plan'. PRC State Council, 2006. http://www.gov.cn/gongbao/content/2006/content_268766.htm.
PRC State Council. 'The 13th Five-Year Plan for Economic and Social Development of the People's Republic of China (2016–2020)'. PRC State Council, 2016. https://en.ndrc.gov.cn/policies/202105/P020210527785800103339.pdf.
PRC State Council. *China's Energy Conditions and Policies*. Beijing: PRC State Council Information Office, 2007.
PRC State Council. *China's Energy Policy 2012*. Beijing: PRC State Council Information Office, 2012.
PRC State Council. *China's National Energy Strategy and Policy*. Beijing: PRC State Council, 2003.
PRC State Council. *Energy in China's New Era*. Beijing: PRC State Council Information Office, 2020.
Pron, Elzbieta Maria. 'China's Energy Diplomacy via the Shanghai Cooperation Organisation'. In *Energy Security and Sustainable Economic Growth in China*, edited by Shujie Yao and Maria Jesus Herrerias, 52–73. London: Palgrave Macmillan 2014.
Provaggi, Alessandro. 'China Development Bank's Financing Mechanisms: Focus on Foreign Investments'. Global Projects Center. Working Paper, Stanford University, 2013.
Putin, Vladimir. 'Speech at the Shanghai Cooperation Organisation Council of Heads of State'. Kremlin, 2006. http://en.kremlin.ru/events/president/transcripts/23643.
Rehn, Cecilia. 'Kazakhstan–China Oil Pipeline Could Start Operating at Its Full Capacity by 2014'. *Energy Global*, 9 November 2012.
Research and Markets. 'Global and China Cobalt Industry Report, 2018–2023'. Report, Research and Markets, 2019.
Ristuccia, Cristiano Andrea. '1935 Sanctions Against Italy: Would Coal and Crude Oil Have Made a Difference'. *European Review of Economic History* 4, no. 1 (2000): 85–110.
Roantree, Anne Marie. 'CNPC, Uzbekistan Tie Up to Develop Mingbulak Oilfield'. *Reuters*, 20 October 2008.
Rone, Jemera. 'Sudan: Oil & War'. *African Political Economy* 30, no. 97 (2003): 504–510.
Rosen, Daniel, and Thilo Hanemann. *China Invests in Europe: Patterns, Impacts and Policy Implications*. New York: Rhodium Group, 2012.
Ruggie, John Gerard. *Multilateralism Matters: The Theory and Praxis of an Institutional Form*. New York: Columbia University Press, 1993.
Ruggie, John. 'Multilateralism: The Anatomy of an Institution'. *International Organization* 46, no. 3 (1992): 561–598.
SCO. 'Declaration on Establishment of SCO'. Shanghai Cooperation Organisation, 2006.
Seaman, John. *Energy Security, Transnational Pipelines and China's Role in Asia*. Paris: Institut Français des Relations Internationales, 2010.
Shen, Wei. 'China-Africa Declaration on Climate Change: Old Wine in New Bottles?', IDS, 2021. https://www.ids.ac.uk/opinions/china-africa-declaration-on-climate-change-old-wine-in-new-bottles/.

Bibliography

Shi, Dan. '我国能源政策回顾与未来的政策' ['China's energy policy and future policy review']. *Economic Research Reference* 20 (2000): 20–27.

Singh, Swaran. 'China's Quest for Multilateralism: Perspectives from India'. *Social and Behavioral Science* 2, no. 5 (2010): 720–729.

Smith, David. 'China Urges Immediate End to Conflict in South Sudan'. *Guardian*, 6 January 2014.

Smyth, Russel, Qingguo Zhai, and Wenguo Hu. 'Restructuring China's Petrochemical Enterprises: A Case Study of the Fushun Petrochemical Company'. *Post-Communist Economies* 13, no. 2 (2001): 243–261.

Snyder, Francis. *The European Union and China, 1949–2008: Basic Documents and Commentary*. Oxford: Hart Publishing, 2009.

Sukhanov, Alexander. 'Caspian Oil Exports Heading East'. *Asian Times*, 9 February 2005.

Swan, James. 'China in Africa: Implications for U.S. Policy'. US Senate Committee on Foreign Relations, 2008. http://www.foreign.senate.gov/imo/media/doc/ChristensenTestimony080604a.pdf.

Tang, Xiaoyang. 'A Brief Analysis of China's Economic and Trade Cooperation Zones in Africa'. *West Asia and Africa* 11 (2010): 17–22.

Taylor, Ian. 'China's Oil Diplomacy in Africa'. *International Affairs* 82, no. 5 (2006): 937–959.

Taylor, Ian. *China and Africa: Engagement and Compromise*. London: Routledge, 2006.

Tian, Chunrong. 'Analysis on Import and Export of Chinese Petroleum in 2002'. *International Petroleum Economics* 3 (2003): 6.

Tian, Shaohui. 'China Focus: What to Expect from Belt and Road Forum'. *Xinhua News*, 1 May 2017.

Tisdall, Simon. 'Irresistible Rise of the Dictators' Club'. *The Guardian*, 6 June 2006.

Tobin, Damian. 'From Maoist Self-Reliance to International Oil Consumer: A Resource-Based Appraisal of the Challenges Facing China's Petrochemical Sector'. *Journal of Chinese Economic & Business Studies* 6, no. 4 (2008): 363–383.

Tønnesson, Stein, and Åshild Kolås. 'Energy Security in Asia: China, India, Oil and Peace'. Working Paper, International Peace Research Institute, 2006.

UN. 'China Headed towards Carbon Neutrality by 2060; President Xi Jinping Vows to Halt New Coal Plants Abroad'. United Nations, 2021.

UNCTAD. 'Country-Specific Lists of Bilateral Investment Treaties'. United Nations Conference on Trade and Development, 2012. http://unctad.org/en/Pages/DIAE/International%20Investment%20Agreements%20%28IIA%29/Country-specific-Lists-of-BITs.aspx.

UNDP. 'World Energy Assessment: Energy and the Challenge of Sustainability'. 2000. https://www.undp.org/sites/g/files/zskgke326/files/publications/World%20Energy%20Assessment-2000.pdf.

UPI. 'China Urges Global Energy Cooperation'. *United Press International*, 16 January 2012. http://www.upi.com/Business_News/Energy-Resources/2012/01/16/China-urges-global-energy-cooperation/UPI-77361326740422.

UPI. 'China Urges Global Energy Cooperation'. *United Press International*, 16 January 2021. http://www.upi.com/Business_News/Energy-Resources/2012/01/16/China-urges-global-energy-cooperation/UPI-77361326740422.

US Congress House. 'Energy as a Weapon: Implications for U.S. Policy'. 2007. https://www.govinfo.gov/content/pkg/CHRG-109hhrg31181/html/CHRG-109hhrg31181.htm.

US DOE. 'Energy Policy Act of 2005 Section 1837: National Security Review of International Energy Requirements'. 2006. https://www.govinfo.gov/content/pkg/PLAW-109publ58/pdf/PLAW-109publ58.pdf.

US DOS. 'Energy Diplomacy in the 21st Century'. 2012. http://www.state.gov/r/pa/pl/2012/200637.htm.
van der Hoeven, Maria. 'IEA Vision on International Energy Governance'. *Energy Strategy Reviews* 1, no. 2 (2012): 73–75.
Walt, Stephen. 'Sino-American Rivalry: A Chinese View'. *Foreign Policy*, 21 November 2011. http://walt.foreignpolicy.com/posts/2011/11/21/sino_american_rivalry_a_chinese_view.
Wan, Zhihong. 'China, Kazakhstan Sign New Gas Pipeline Deal'. *China Daily*, 14 June 2010.
Wang, Zhuwei. 'Securing Energy Flows from Central Asia to China: Relevance of the Energy Charter Treaty'. Brussel: Energy Charter Secretariat, 2014.
Weiss, Thomas, and Thakur Ramesh. *The UN and Global Governance: An Idea and Its Prospects*. Bloomington: Indiana University Press, 2010.
Weitz, Richard. 'Shanghai Summit Fails to Yield NATO-style Defence Agreement'. *Jane's Intelligence Review* 18, no. 8 (2006): 40–43.
White House. 'The National Security Strategy'. 2006. https://www.comw.org/qdr/fulltext/nss2006.pdf.
Wong, Jacqueline. 'KazMunaiGas in Deal to tap Urikhtau Gas Field'. *Reuters*, 23 February 2011.
World Bank. 'World Bank and AIIB Sign Cooperation Framework'. World Bank, 2017. https://www.worldbank.org/en/news/press-release/2017/04/23/world-bank-and-aiib-sign-cooperation-framework.
World Bank. 'World Bank Enterprise Survey'. World Bank, 2021. https://www.enterprisesurveys.org/en/enterprisesurveys.
Wu, Xuxin. '經濟全球化下中亞石油國際合作和中國石油國際合作之比較' [Comparison between Sino-Central Asian oil cooperation with China's international oil cooperation under the globalized economy]. *Journal of Shengli Oilfield Party School* 19, no. 1 (2006): 101–103.
Xi, Jinping. '国家中长期经济社会发展战略若干重大问题' [Major issues in the national medium- to long-term economic and social development strategy], *Qiushi*, 31 October 2020. http://www.xinhuanet.com/politics/leaders/2020-10/31/c_1126681658.htm.
Xing, Guangcheng. 《上海合作组织发展报告2009》 [Shanghai Cooperation Organization Development Report 2009]. Beijing: CASS Publishing.
Xinhua News. 'China Not Seeking to Move Outdated Capacity Abroad', *Xinhua News*, 20 May 2015. http://www.china.org.cn/business/2015-05/20/content_35617344.htm.
Xinhua News. 'Kazakhstan-China Oil Pipeline Opens to Operation'. *Xinhua News*, 12 July 2008.
Xinhua News. 'Memorabilia of Chinese Presidents' Visits in Africa'. *Xinhua News*, 24 March 2013. http://news.xinhuanet.com/world/2013-03/24/c_124496931.htm.
Xinhua News. 'Scientific Outlook on Development'. *China Daily*, 8 September 2010.
Xinhua News. 'Xi Announces 10 Major Programs to Boost China-Africa Cooperation in Coming 3 Years'. *Xinhua News*, 4 December 2015.
Xinhua News. '国务院常务会议原则通过《能源中长期发展规划纲要》' ['Energy and Long-Term Development Plan' approved in State Council executive meeting]. *Xinhua News*, 1 July 2004. http://news.xinhuanet.com/zhengfu/2004-07/01/content_1559228.htm.
Xu, Qinhua. 'China's Energy Diplomacy and its Implications for Global Energy Security'. FES Briefing Paper, 2007. http://library.fes.de/pdf-files/iez/global/04763.pdf.
Yergin, Danial. 'Energy Security in the 1990s'. *Foreign Affairs* 67, no. 1 (1988):110–132.
Yu, Kaho. 'Energy Cooperation in the Belt and Road Initiative: EU Experience of the Trans-European Networks for Energy'. *Asia Europe Journal* 16, no. 3 (2018): 251–265.

Yu, Kaho. 'Energy Cooperation under the Belt and Road Initiative: Implications for Global Energy Governance'. *The Journal of World Investment & Trade* 20: no. 2–3 (2019).
Yu, Kaho. 'The Geopolitics of Energy Cooperation in China's Belt and Road Initiative'. *NBR Special Report* 68 (2017): 29–39.
Yu, Kaho. 'Critical Minerals Strategy of Asia-Pacific Countries: Diversification, Circular Economy and Multilateral Initiatives'. In *Geoeconomics of Decarbonisation in Asia Pacific*, edited by KAS, 8–27. Berlin: Konrad-Adenauer-Stiftung, 2022.
Yueh, Linda. 'China's "Going Out, Bringing In" Policy: The Geo-Economics of China's Rise'. *IISS Seminar*, 23–25 March 2012.
Zeng, Peiyan. Speech at BOAO Forum for Asia, Beijing, 26–27 November 2012.
Zha, Daojiong, and Suetyi Lai. 'EU-China Energy Governance: What Lessons to Be Drawn?' In *Challenges of European External Energy Governance with Emerging Powers*, edited by Michele Knodt and Nadine Piefer, 129–138. Surrey: Ashgate, 2015.
Zha, Daojiong, and Weixing Hu. 'Promoting Energy Partnership in Beijing and Washington'. *Washington Quarterly* 30, no. 4 (2007): 105–115.
Zha, Daojiong. 'China's Energy Security: Domestic and International Issues'. *Survival: Global Politics and Strategy* 48, no. 1 (2006): 179–90.
Zha, Daojiong. '中国石油安全的国际政治经济学分析' [Analysis of the international political economy of China's oil security]. Beijing: Contemporary World Publisher, 2005.
Zhang, Chao. 'The EU-China Energy Cooperation'. Briefing Paper, EIAS, 2017.
Zhang, Guobao. Speech in The Observer Forum 2010, Beijing, 1 January 2011.
Zhang, X. '中欧能源合作的未来——基于能源安全与气候变化的分析' [Future of Sino-EU cooperation: Analysis base on energy security and climate change]. *International Economic Cooperation* 3 (2012): 11–16.
Zhu, Feng. 'A High Price to Pay: China's Resource Diplomacy Requires Wisdom'. *New Finance*, 18 May 2005. http://media.163.com/05/0518/10/1K1FC60A00141A16.html.
Zoellick, Rober B. 'Whither China: From Membership to Responsibility? (Remarks to National Committee on U.S.-China Relations)'. US Department of State, 2005. https://2001-2009.state.gov/s/d/former/zoellick/rem/53682.htm.
Zweig, Daivd, and Mikkal Herberg. 'China's Energy Rise, the US, and the New Geopolitics of Energy'. *Pacific Council on International Policy* (2010): 35–74.
Zweig, David, and Bi Jianhai. 'China's Global Hunt for Energy'. *Foreign Affairs* 8, no. 5 (2005): 25–38.
Zweig, David. 'A New "Trading State" Meets the Developing World'. Working Paper no. 31, Center on China's Transnational Relations of the Hong Kong University of Science and Technology.

Interviews Conducted by the Author

A Beijing-based think tank, interview with the author, 2013.
A former Chinese oil company researcher, interview with the author, 2014.
A former officer of a China-Europe joint clean energy centre, interview with the author, 2013.
A former officer of an international energy organisation, interview with the author, 2014.
Keunwook Paik, senior fellow at Chatham House, interview with the author, 2018.
Yishan Xia, senior fellow at the China Institute of International Studies, interview with the author, 2021.